Capital Compounders

How to Beat the Market and Make Money Investing in Growth Stocks

Revised & Expanded
Second Edition

Robin R. Speziale

National Bestselling Author, *Market Masters*

r.speziale@gmail.com | RobinSpeziale.com

DISCLAIMER

CONTENTS

START HERE

Thank you for reading *Capital Compounders*. If you have the eBook version, please pick-up the Paperback on Amazon too – *I think it will look great on your bookshelf!*

I've been picking stocks since 2005, and it's certainly been a fun, humbling, and rewarding journey. Along the way I write books, blogs, newsletters, and do other things to help you – the DIY Investor – on your own journey.

Learn More:

✪ READ: *Market Masters*, *Blog*

✪ SUBSCRIBE: *Newsletter*, *YouTube Channel*

✪ JOIN: *Club*, *Patreon*

✪ CONTACT: *Email*, *Twitter*

Go to RobinSpeziale.com for all of this and more…

"Whatever the mind of man can conceive and believe, it can achieve" – Napoleon Hill

INTRODUCTION

I love the stock market. It's like a treasure hunt – digging deep, trying to find the winning stocks among all the others. I've been investing in stocks since 2005 (13+ years), and building wealth throughout this fascinating, humbling, and rewarding journey. I'm just like you – a Do-it-Yourself (DIY) Investor – and similar to most DIY investors, Warren Buffett was my first teacher. But then I discovered Philip Fisher and Peter Lynch, and their respective books; *Common Stocks and Uncommon Profits,* and *One Up On Wall Street.* So while value investing provided me with a foundation early on, it was both Fisher and Lynch's teachings on growth investing that shaped me, and my stock portfolio for years to come. I don't see this changing in the foreseeable future. I am a growth investor.

Investing in publicly-traded growth companies helped me build a $300,000+ portfolio before 30. Today it's closer to $500,000 and my portfolio goal for age 35 is $1,000,000. Interestingly, if I can maintain a 15% compound annual return in my portfolio from age 30 – 85 (55 years), that $1,000,000 can turn into $1,000,000,000 (yes – possibly $1 Billion!). That's without the infusion of new money – from capital appreciation alone. Compounding is a wonderful thing. In reality this is wishful thinking. Building wealth takes patience, and one must remain active in the market and allocate capital to new wealth-creating opportunities over time, in order to continually achieve an above average compound return. But I'm a dreamer.

How a 15% Compound Annual Return Can Turn $500,000 into $1,000,000,000 in 55 Years (rough math – portfolio doubles every ~ 5 years using the rule of 72):

Age	Portfolio
30	$500,000
35	$1,000,000
40	$2,000,000
45	$4,000,000
50	$8,000,000
55	$16,000,000
60	$32,000,000
65	$64,000,000
70	$128,000,000
75	$256,000,000
80	$512,000,000
85	$1,024,000,000

For starters, what I will share with you in this book is how you can also build an achievable $300,000+ portfolio (and possibly more), by investing intelligently in growth stocks. *Anyone* can make money in stocks; the market doesn't care about the colour of your skin, your culture, or sex. However, there's some important things you need to first learn about the stock market, otherwise you'll find yourself fighting in a treacherous battlefield. You must not only master the market, but most important – your own doubts, biases, and behaviour. I wrote this book to be the guide in your DIY investing journey.

If you've been reading my free investment newsletter on RobinSpeziale.com/Subscribe (there's 3,500+ subscribers; join now!), you'll know that I call the top growth stocks "Capital Compounders". Stocks that double, then double again, and again… achieving tenbagger ($1 turns into $10), 100-bagger ($1 turns into $100), and 100+ bagger returns. Think Apple, Netflix, and Amazon.

Investing in future Capital Compounders is the goal. But let's be honest – it can tough. There's so many stocks (1,000s) trading on multiple exchanges, in various countries around the world. Plus, identifying a future Capital Compounder is not a binary process, where if a company checks off all of *these* boxes it's a winner, and if it doesn't, it's a loser. Most Capital Compounder companies start out as new ideas, centered around a disruptive product and / or service, with a pioneering Founder / CEO at the helm who successfully executes the company's grand but achievable vision. But by no means is this *the* definitive mix of winning factors. Bagging the big winners is not formulaic, nor is it easy.

The discovery, and stock selection process involves a whole lot of intuition and luck, as much as it requires intellect and hard work. Imagine buying Amazon in 1997 (IPO), and having both the conviction and wherewithal to hold the stock through its ups and downs (-50% + drops in the stock in multiple years). You would have had to either be crazy, genius, or you simply forgot to login to your brokerage account for all those years. But holding Amazon from 1997 until 2018 would have made you a multimillionaire. That's why investing is more an art than it is a science, and why it's possible that virtually anyone can make money in the stock market – sometimes the most unassuming ones.

Luckily for me, successful investing doesn't require a Mathematics degree, 180 IQ, or any special certifications (e.g. CFA). This is not widely known but many of the world's top investors do not hold conventional degrees for the world of finance. You will find B.A.s (Bachelor of Arts) among the degrees of famous investors, and hedge fund managers. Case in point: Warren Buffett earned a B.A. in economics, and then was rejected for enrollment by the Harvard Business School. "I spent 10 minutes with the Harvard alumnus who was doing the interview, and he assessed my capabilities and turn me down", said Buffett years after being rejected by Harvard. Today, Warren Buffett's net worth is north of $90 Billion, making him one of the richest people in the world. These are some of the other notable investors who hold ("only") a B.A. degree:

- Bill Gross (B.A. in psychology)
- George Soros (B.A. in philosophy)
- Carl Icahn (B.A. in philosophy)
- Peter Lynch (B.A. in history, psychology, classics, and philosophy)
- Bill Ackman (B.A. in history)

I repeat – *anyone* can make money in stocks. But the top investors continually pick more winners than losers, beat the market over time, and stick through the good times and the bad times in the market.

I'll cover some of the top growth investors' principles, and investing strategies through this book that you can apply in the stock market. You will also learn what the commonalities are among today's top growth stocks (Small / Mid / Large Caps), and emerging growth stocks (Micro Caps) so that you can more easily find the future Capital Compounders – whether that's in 2018 (when this book was published), 2020, or 2050.

For background, I gave this book the same title as my talk from the Fairfax Financial Shareholder's Dinner (April, 2017), where I shared with the audience my selection of 25 market-beating stocks (*Capital Compounders*) and their outstanding managers / owner-operators ("capital allocators"). This outperforming group of companies had over the long run (average 15+ public years) compounded capital at exceptionally high rates, in turn generating vast amounts of wealth for their shareholders. You'll find that original talk in this book, as well as my follow-up – "Next Capital Compounders" – where I introduce an additional 15 stocks to round-up the list to 40 Capital Compounders.

You will also find the most popular writings from my newsletter – "My 72 Rules", "How I Pick Winners", "100-Baggers", "Small-Cap Ideas", and "Small Companies; Big Dreams", among others. Plus, I've included material from my very first book – *Lessons from the Successful Investor (2010)*, combined with real-life stories, and experiences from my journey as a DIY investor. Remember; it's been 13 years, and along the way, I have met a lot of other very interesting DIY investors, who share some of their own stories, and growth investing strategies later in this book.

As a bonus, I reveal "My Universe of Growth Stocks"; seven (7) Model Portfolios – Capital Compounders, Future 60 Small Companies, Chinese Technology (and their U.S. Equivalents), Great Canadian Technology, U.S. Disruptors and Innovators, Cannabis Companies, and Robotics /AI / Automation – that contain actual stocks in my portfolio and watchlist that can help guide you while you build upon, or start your portfolio for the first time.

I hope that you enjoy my book, *Capital Compounders*, and that it's entertaining (because finance can be dry), as well as informative. I've packed in as many tips and tricks that you can apply in the stock market as soon as you are done reading the book cover to cover. But you can also dip in and out, skipping chapters, and coming back as you wish. If you have the eBook version of the book, please pick-up the Paperback on Amazon too – I think it will look great on your bookshelf! Plus, you an easily dog-ear it, and highlight any key points.

What You'll Learn:

- How you can turn $0 into $300,000 (and more) by saving, and then investing in growth stocks. I did it in only 12 years (but you might get there sooner)
- Why growth investing is better than value investing
- What top growth stocks ("Capital Compounders") have in common and how to find the next Capital Compounders in the stock market
- How I pick winning stocks (including sharing with you my 7 growth model portfolios)

- Actual examples of tenbagger and 100-bagger stocks, including the top 30 super stocks from the past 30 years – some stocks might surprise you!

- My 72 Rules; winning in the market, managing a portfolio, avoiding the losers and value traps, and becoming a better long term investor

- Growth investing strategies from top growth investors Peter Lynch, Philip Fisher, William O'Neil, Joel Greenblatt, and Thomas Rowe Price Jr.

- 75+ events, and corporate developments that move stocks, and 50+ predictions for the future

- How a hedge fund manager achieved a 24% compound annual return (since 1998!)

- Exclusive interviews with a small-cap technology analyst, and a growth hedge fund manager

- How to decode market psychology, and control your own behavioural biases

- My daily routine – how I stay on top of the stock market, and find new growth opportunities

- 100+ Free DIY investor resources (my favourites)

How to Get the Most Out of This Book:

- Make it yours. Highlight the most important things that you learn. Dog-ear this book. Jot crucial points into a notepad. Come back to concepts later

- Take breaks. Stop throughout and think: How can *this* make me money in the market? When will I apply it? What stocks should I add to my watchlist?

- Go back. After you've read *Capital Compounders* once, read it a second time, and then a third whenever you feel the need for guidance

- Pay it forward. Share this book with a relative, friend, or colleague to help them on their journey
- Continually build your knowledge base; read my book recommendations, and sign up to my free newsletter (RobinSpeziale.com/Subscribe)

Email me anytime if you have questions or comments about the book (r.speziale@gmail.com). Happy Investing!

– Robin Speziale (October, 2018)

CHAPTER 1

HOW I BUILT A $300,000+ STOCK PORTFOLIO BEFORE 30 (AND HOW YOU CAN TOO!) MY 8-STEP WEALTH BUILDING JOURNEY

When I was 12 years old I made a decision. I was going to be rich. I looked up to successful people and wanted what they had: financial freedom. They seemed to be happier than everyone else. But who was I kidding? Becoming rich would be an uphill battle. I was from a middle-class family of humble means. There was no trust fund. And my parents didn't have work connections to land me my first job. The odds were stacked against me. But I still made the decision to be rich and start on my wealth-building journey. The path I chose to get me there: Do-it-Yourself Investing, "DIY Investing".

Today, I manage a $500,000 stock portfolio. I'm 31, and my stock portfolio grows by the day. As I said in the introduction, my goal is $1,000,000 in stocks by the time I'm 35, and $1 Billion by 85 (yes – call me crazy!). I'll show you my 8-step wealth building journey and how you can start building wealth by investing in stocks too.

Step 1: Study Successful Investors

I realized that if I wanted to make money in stocks I had to first study successful stock investors. Common sense, right? Isaac Newton said it best: "If I have seen further than others, it is by standing upon the shoulders of giants." So, from age 12 to 20, I read around 50 books on Business / Investing. I was a very frequent visitor to both my local library and Chapters book store.

These were the top 10 most important investing books for me early on, and ones that I recommend you read:

1. The Intelligent Investor, Benjamin Graham

It was through *The Intelligent Investor* that I was introduced to value investing, and the essential concepts of "Margin of Safety", "Mr. Market", and "Intrinsic Value", among others. Warren Buffett called Graham's tome "the best book on investing ever written". While I'm not a so-called value investor, this book is still foundational and you can treat it as 'Investing 101'.

2. Common Stocks and Uncommon Profits, Philip Fisher

Philip Fisher opened up my world to growth stocks. After reading *Common Stocks and Uncommon Profits*, I started paying more for higher quality, and faster growing companies trading on the stock market.

3. One Up On Wall Street, Peter Lynch

There are so many easy-to-implement lessons in *One up on Wall Street*. But what stuck with me was Peter Lynch's focus on "buying what you know". That lesson saved me from investing in many stocks that I didn't fully understand (e.g. Valeant). Also, I was inspired by Peter Lynch's insatiable drive to invest in "tenbaggers" (10x return), which we'll explore more in this book.

4. Market Wizards, Jack D. Schwager

Jack D. Schwager introduced me to some of America's top traders in *Market Wizards*. But instead of just writing about those traders' favourite stock picks (what they buy) he explained their trading frameworks (why and how they buy), which was invaluable to me.

5. Buffettology, Mary Buffett and David Clark

There are many books that try to explain how Warren Buffett invests in stocks but most come up short. *Buffettology* was the book that got it right, in my opinion, with many actionable ideas that prove Warren Buffett wasn't always the boring investor that he is today.

6. The Money Masters, John Train

A classic that was diverse and fun to read, *The Money Masters* shares strategies from some of the world's top investors – it's got lots of 'dog-ears' after all these years.

7. The Essays of Warren Buffett, Lawrence A. Cunningham

Lawrence A. Cunningham compiled Warren Buffett's priceless teachings from Berkshire Hathaway's annual reports in this comprehensive compilation. Mr. Cunningham would later endorse my book, *Market Masters (2016)*, on the front cover – thanks Lawrence!

8. A Random Walk Down Wall Street, Burton G. Malkiel

If you're a DIY Investor like me, then you likely believe that the market is *not* efficient, meaning you can beat its returns over time. But Burton Malkiel argues that the market *is* efficient. Though I don't totally agree with the "Efficient Market Theory", it's important to understand both sides of the coin. Plus, Burton Malkiel has lots of great thoughts, and stories on the stock market.

9. Poor Charlie's Almanack, Peter D Kaufman

Warren Buffett's partner, Charlie Munger, influenced Buffett to invest in companies with strong competitive advantages, albeit at higher valuations. *Poor Charlie's Almanack* is packed with wise advice on investing, and life in general – Munger does not mince his words.

10. The Snowball, Alice Schroeder

Alice Schroeder chronicles the most important capitalist of our time – Warren Buffett – in *The Snowball*. It goes without saying that Buffett is the reason many people, including myself, were initially inspired to invest in stocks. He's a role model. The book also has never-before-seen photos that reveal Buffett's personal life – family, friends.

Early on, I also studied Forbes' list of the 500 Richest People in the World and Canadian Business' Richest Canadians. Picking up these magazines became an annual tradition. It then all became very clear to me: I would become rich by earning money, saving the proceeds (what's left over), and then investing in stocks as other rich people, such as Warren Buffett had done long before me.

Step 2: Earn and Save Money When You Are Young

I opened my first bank account when I was about 8 years old. As you can imagine, there wasn't much there; cash from birthdays, Christmas, and random chores. Maybe $500 in total from what I can remember. I had to earn and save more money fast! So I did what Warren Buffett had done at my age – delivered newspapers. At 12, I joined PennySaver and became a paperboy for three neighborhoods in my hometown of Mississauga, Canada. I deposited each pay cheque, along with any other money straight into my savings account. I can't emphasize enough how important it is to save. If you can't save; you can't invest; and you can't build wealth. Today I try to save 40% of my take-home pay. Years ago, I remember reading an interesting story about Curt Degerman, nick-named *Tin-Can-Curt*. Tin-Can-Curt lived in a small town in Sweden his whole life, rummaging through trash bins for tin cans. With the money he earned from selling those tin cans as scrap metal, Tin-Can-Curt invested in stocks. At age 60, Tin-Can-Curt suffered a debilitating heart attack, taking his life. Shortly after, his will was made public. Tin-Can-Curt's family was surprised to learn that their eccentric, homeless relative had amassed $1.1 million in stocks. I'm not saying that you should live like Tin-Can-Curt, but rather that one must save their money to then invest in order to build wealth. Tin-Can-Curt proves it doesn't take much because of the power of compound returns...

Step 3: Understand How to Compound Money

Once I turned 14 and started high school, my savings account had grown to around $5,000. At that point, I wanted to invest in stocks. But because of my age (under 18), I wasn't eligible to open a brokerage account. So I started with bonds that I got at my local bank branch – CIBC. After returning home from the bank, I placed those newly purchased Canadian Savings Bonds into a small but sturdy wooden box, hiding it safely under my bed. I was so proud. I knew that my bonds would generate interest for me on the principal amount ($5,000). "Compound interest is like magic", I thought, and "the earlier I start investing money the longer my money will compound ('work') for me". Throughout high school, I worked several odd-jobs (mechanic shop janitor, meat department clerk, salesperson, painter, and Best Buy associate), all the while saving money from each pay cheque, and then buying more bonds to further compound my money.

While I couldn't open a stock brokerage account (too young), I took the opportunity to practice investing in the stock market while still in high school. It was through a stock market challenge organized by Andrew Tai's *Investors of Tomorrow* where I put my amateur investing skills to the test, winning 1st place nationwide in 2005. Mississauga News reported:

"Robin Speziale, a grade twelve student at Erindale Secondary School in Mississauga, Ontario captured victory with a final portfolio value of $207,977.34, approximately a 108% return on investment. His win was largely attributed to investments in embattled biotech company Elan Corporation PLC (NYSE: ELN). After Elan stock suffered a crushing fall early on in the competition due to regulatory problems, Speziale purchased shares, which fell to as low as $3.00 from over $30.00. Anticipating a rebound, he held his position through to the end of the competition where Elan closed at $6.23 on May 6, 2005. Shares of Elan currently trade near $8.00."

Curious, I looked up Elan's stock price years later and discovered that in 2013 it had been acquired by Perrigo for $8.6 Billion ($16.50/share), representing a close-to tripling since the end of the competition. But if I had actually bought Elan stock for $3.00/share, and then held until it got bought out at $16.50/share, I would have made over 5 times my investment; a 5-bagger! At this point, I was so excited to actually start investing in the "real" stock market...

Step 4: Invest in Stocks for the Long Run

I turned 18, and was ready to enter University (party time! — NOT). In September, 2005, I moved into my cozy on-campus dorm room at the University of Waterloo (UW), a 1-hour drive from my hometown of Mississauga. At this point I finally opened my first stock brokerage account. I could now invest in the stock market. At University, while everyone else was tracking sports stats and watching game highlights, I was screening stocks and reading annual reports. Investing in stocks was a 'no-brainer' for me because I could compound my investment returns through both capital appreciation (stock price goes up) and dividend income (quarterly dividend payouts from companies).

I had already cashed out of my bonds (worth $10,000 at this point), and invested that money evenly into 5 stocks; $2,000 stake in each company. I felt like a true capitalist. This is how my idols Benjamin Graham, Philip Fisher, Peter Lynch, and Warren Buffett got rich; by investing in stocks. As I earned money though UW co-op jobs (which I recommend to every young person), and continually bought more stocks, my portfolio grew, and grew, and grew. I was on top of the world. Then the financial crisis (2007/2008) happened...

Step 5: Capitalize on Crises in the Market

I was 21 when the entire world ended in 2008 (or so

most people thought at the time). The financial crisis thrust economies around the world into recession, and stock markets collapsed in lock-step. My stock portfolio imploded, suffering a close-to 50% decline from peak to trough. The financial press was all doom and gloom; "Sell! Sell! Sell!" Most people were scared silly and sold out of all of their stocks to hoard cash. What did I do? I gathered up any new cash, and invested everything into the existing stocks in my portfolio. I was buying stocks in 2008 when most people were selling (crazy, right?).

Honestly, when I pulled the buy trigger when stocks were still in free-fall, I was scared stiff. But I'm glad I made that move as my stocks would soon rebound off the March 2009 bottom, pushing way above pre-financial crisis highs into the years to come. I bought quality stocks on sale – 50% off! Was I a young genius; able to time the market? No. I simply learned from Benjamin Graham that economies operate in cycles, and that markets have mood swings, which he personified in "Mr. Market". Graham explained that patient investors could capitalize on bipolar markets by buying stocks on sale, rather than becoming fearful and flee because markets would soon become euphoric again. It's a never ending manic-depressive cycle.

I stayed invested in the market, and even bought more stocks because I understood it would be costly to leave. Not only can you miss prolonged run-ups in the market, but significant short-term advances too that can be incredibly rewarding. Based on the analysis that I conducted in *Lessons From The Successful Investor*, from 1871 to 2009 (138 years) the S&P 500 delivered positive returns 72% of the time and negative returns only 28% of the time. That means that for every ten-year time horizon, you can expect seven years of positive returns and just three years of negative returns. These S&P 500 findings are similar to the TSX Composite, where being in the Canadian market through its ups and downs also pays off in the long run. From 1934 to 2014, the TSX compounded at a 9.8% annual return, and so over that 80-year period, an investment in Canadian stocks had grown 1,597-fold despite 13 recessions, double-digit interest rates, and world crises.

Of course, in hindsight 2009 was a great year to be an investor as it is in every recession, bear market, or correction, where even great growth stocks fall in price. I would later make a similar move years later in February, 2016 to capitalize on a bear market in Canadian stocks, after the TSX Composite declined -25% from its high in September, 2014. Why so confident? I knew that the average bear market on the TSX (Toronto Stock Exchange) experienced -28% losses, lasting 9 months, while the average bull market advanced +124%, lasting 50 months. Based on that historical data since 1956, I estimated that taking on risk after a -25% decline would eventually be rewarded in the long run by investing in cheaper stocks during bear markets, as bull markets have proven to outperform and outlast bear markets.

Step 6: Manage and Refine Your Stock Portfolio

In 2010, upon graduating from the University of Waterloo, my stock portfolio had grown to $50,000. More money than any of my friends who mostly incurred debt from all of their student loans, and spent their money on beer, going out, and the newest clothes and gadgets. This was certainly an inflection point for me as the magic of compounding started to take real effect. Plus, I was just about to enter a full time career and earn a much bigger pay cheque (plus bonus), which meant more money for stocks.

By 2013, three years into my first full time job, my stock portfolio grew to $125,000. However, I realized that I could build wealth faster if I compounded returns at a higher rate. A 15% compound annual return was my new goal because based on the rule of 72 I could double my money every 5 years. So, at 25 I made it my mission to build a stock portfolio that could actually beat the market consistently over time. The S&P 500 and S&P/TSX were my index benchmarks – the ones to beat. (Note: Warren Buffett wrote a paper that doesn't get much attention, on why some investors beat the market, while others don't: "Superinvestors of Graham-and-Doddsville". I read this paper to give me early encouragement).

I started to watch BNN Market Call, and various shows on CNBC, as well as re-read classic investment books (some of which I shared earlier), pouring over magazines (MoneySense, Canadian MoneySaver, Canadian Business), newspapers (Globe and Mail's Report on Business, and Financial Post), clicking through websites (Bloomberg.com, BNN.ca), as well as following the top investors from around the world. At that point, I decided to become a growth investor, and invest in growth companies that could compound returns over the long run. I was tired of sitting on the sidelines, watching "expensive" growth stocks go up, while "cheap" value stocks got cheaper. I learned that "expensive" stocks could easily, and quickly become more expensive after continuous earnings beats. I also learned not to listen to the Bears (naysayers), who project their pessimism onto the market and you. As the saying goes; even a broken clock is right twice a day. My new world was growth stocks; companies and founders that were changing the world, and making it a better place to live, work, and play. Quality stocks.

Step 7: Stick to Your Investment Strategy

Since the start of my DIY investing journey, I have continued to earn, save, and invest in stocks using the same growth investing strategy, which I'll explain throughout this book. Before 30, I turned $10,000 into $300,000. And now at age 31 I manage a $500,000 stock portfolio thanks to my growth stocks, and their market-beating returns.

With a larger capital base, it's amazing how much more rapidly my portfolio can compound wealth for me. For example, a 10% return will thrust my portfolio to $550,000 within the next year, without adding any new money – on capital appreciation alone. I say "10%" because over the long run (since 1934), the TSX has delivered a 9.8% annual compound return, despite recessions, bear markets, and world crises. In fact, $1,000 (one-time) invested in the Canadian market in 1934 would have grown to over $2,5000,000 by 2018 with 9.8% annual compound returns. That's "magic", in my world. The historical returns of the S&P 500 and Dow Jones Industrial Average are even better, which is why I also invest in U.S. stocks and use both of those indexes as benchmarks too.

Also, I benefited by starting young, and so you should start investing as soon as possible. I was able to make "cheap" mistakes, losing money without worrying about putting food on the table, or a roof over my head. Certainly, it's best to make many mistakes early, and to make those mistakes often so that you can learn, adapt, and push on, refining your strategy over time. But that's not to say it's too late if you're just starting in the stock market at age 30, 40, or 50. My advice: start now (no excuses!).

Step 8: Continually Learn and Grow as an Investor

My DIY investing journey has been fun so far. But I also know that I can improve my odds of success by continually learning, and experiencing the market – all of its ups and downs, wins, and losses. That is why in 2015 I contacted, and met with 28 of Canada's Top Investors, who collectively manage billions of dollars in their funds, and personal accounts. Those top investors revealed to me how they invest in stocks, sharing all of their proven investment strategies that I could then apply in the stock market, and improve my own returns. It was an invaluable experience, which is why I put all of that investment advice into a book – *Market Masters* – that released in 2016 around the world. I've included some content from *Market Masters* throughout this book that I think will help you.

My 8-Step Wealth Building Journey (Re-cap):

1. Study Successful Investors
2. Earn and Save Money When You Are Young
3. Understand How to Compound Money
4. Invest in Stocks for the Long Run
5. Capitalize on Crises in the Market
6. Manage and Refine Your Stock Portfolio
7. Stick to Your Investment Strategy
8. Continually Learn and Grow as an Investor

✪ CHAPTER 2 ✪
GROWTH INVESTING VS. VALUE INVESTING

Before moving on, here's a quick overview of "growth investing" in comparison to "value investing", highlighting why I think being a growth investor is the better choice in the long run to build wealth. I personally grew tired of sitting on the sidelines, watching growth stocks get more expensive (go up), while my value stocks did nothing or lost money. It's like that saying; "you get what you pay for". If you're well versed in growth vs. value, you can skip this chapter and move on to chapter 3 – *My 72 Rules*.

Growth investors will invest in stocks that have higher-than-average return potential compared to other stocks in the market. That means growth investors use criteria such as revenue growth, earnings growth, book value growth, return on equity (ROE), and return on invested capital (ROIC), among other metrics to inform their investment decisions. Important definition: *Return on Equity (ROE)* is calculated by dividing a business's net income by its book value (assets – liabilities). "Book value" is also known as equity or shareholders equity. ROE is the measure of management's effectiveness at generating income from their shareholder's capital base, and is akin to a mutual fund manager pooling together $100,000 of his clients' money, and in the first year, generating a 20% ($20,000) return. So shareholders expect management to wisely allocate their money into growth opportunities that will achieve the highest return possible.

Rationally minded investors will be attracted to companies with high ROE, because they want to invest their money where there will be the greatest return. Return on Invested Capital (ROIC), which I prefer to use, and which will be talked about throughout this book, incorporates long term debt back into the denominator.

But these criteria – revenue growth, earnings growth, book value growth, and high ROE, and ROIC – are just numbers. Successful businesses are constantly innovating, launching new products and services, and expanding into new markets. Also, company management is continually making wise capital allocation decisions, deploying free cash flow (operating cash flow – capital expenditures) to re-investment opportunities, intelligent acquisitions, and share buybacks, to create shareholder value over the long run. (Note: when companies buy back shares they effectively decrease their total common share count. As a result, their earnings per share rises, as the denominator – common shares outstanding – drops).

A company like Coca-Cola doesn't really need smart management, as its growth is near peak-level and so now the company essentially tracks inflation. Whereas a smaller company lives or dies by its management's strategy and ability to execute on a grand, but achievable vision.

Investors can generate astronomically high returns in new companies that have a long runway to grow, such as Amazon, which started trading in 1997. However, the law of large numbers often means that growth stocks' compound returns decrease over time (later in their business cycle), and so the once exceptional performance achieved by growth stocks can stall. Think about Amazon; it can't grow at 25%+ compound returns forever. It's currently a $1 trillion market capitalization company (2018). At that rate (25% growth) it would take over the world very soon. That is why growth investors are always on the lookout to allocate their money into new emerging growth stocks that can deliver high compound returns until those stocks, too, face a slow-down in growth.

The obvious risk associated with growth investing is that investors can "chase hot stocks," effectively buying high and selling low, or over a long period paying a hefty amount in total commissions and fees from excessive turnover (actively buying and selling stocks) in their portfolio. Though, ultimately the risk / reward concept means that growth investors should theoretically be rewarded for their assumption of greater risk in the market with higher returns, and more winners.

Growth stocks exist in the micro-cap, small-cap, and mid-cap segments of the market, because as previously alluded to, growth usually stalls past ~ $100B market cap due to the law of large numbers. High compound returns can't last forever. (Note: Big Tech – "FAANG" stocks – have still been *the* growth stocks to own the past 5 years, but generally smaller companies grow at higher rates over the long run). These are the segments of the stock market:

- Micro-cap: 0 to $100 million

- Small-cap: $100 million – $2 billion

- Mid-cap: $2 billion – $10 billion

- Large-cap: $10 billion – $150 billion

- Mega-cap: $150 billion or more

Investing in growth stocks is the winning strategy if you can wisely pick companies early on that will compound capital over the long run, warding off competitors with superior products and services, increasing market share.

Value investors, on the other hand, will seek out and invest in undervalued stocks. "Undervalued" simply means that those "value stocks" trade below their intrinsic value – the actual worth of a business. That mispricing – a stock's price trading below its intrinsic value – can occur for a variety of reasons, namely company sentiment, unusual or short-term events, and broad market declines. Intrinsic value is a culmination of a company's brands, tangibles, intangibles (including technology and patents), future earnings, and competitive advantage, among other things. Intrinsic value is seen as a better gauge of a company's worth than merely its book value (assets – liabilities), because arguably book value does not adequately account for the true worth of a company.

When I met Fund Manager, Francis Chou, he told me: "Most [value] investors invest in terms of premium or discount to book. That is a serious mistake. Let's say the year was 2006. You examine the loan portfolio [of a U.S. bank] and see all the junk there. As a result, you wouldn't touch a U.S. bank with a barge pole."

Value investors invest in these undervalued value stocks in the anticipation that their market price will revert to their mean price, aligning back to intrinsic value. The problem is that value investors can wait a very long time for this to happen, and that a stock's market price may continue to decline or be volatile. The value investor is saying, "the market is wrong, and I am right".

The biggest risk then in value investing is what is referred to as a value trap, in which a value investor misjudges a stock's intrinsic value. The pain from a value trap is incurred later on, after which a company's fundamentals completely deteriorate, validating the stock's initial cheap price as it continues to drop lower. For this reason, value investors must identify a catalyst, for example; a change in management, to determine whether a stock will actually revert back to its intrinsic value.

Some value investors call themselves "Contrarians", and go so far as to always go against "the herd", betting that the majority is wrong each and every time. This is dangerous. Contrarians who actually beat the market cannot simply, and indiscriminately buy when others sell and sell when others buy. They'd quickly lose a lot of money.

Both the concept and application of value investing have changed over the years since Benjamin Graham popularized the philosophy in *The Intelligent Investor*. Benjamin Graham would seek out and buy a dollar's worth of tangible assets for 50 cents. Value investing has evolved because tangible assets are not as prevalent in companies today as they were in the decades from 1890 to 1980, when industrial, transportation, chemical, steel, textile, and oil and gas companies represented the majority of the stock market. Today, an investor cannot simply "buy a dollar's worth of assets for 50 cents," since most companies that make up the stock market do not consist entirely of *tangible* assets, but rather to a greater extent, *intangible* assets.

Intangible assets include – but are not limited to – trademarks, copyrights, technology, patents, and brands. Notable examples of predominantly intangible companies are Google, Netflix, and Salesforce. Success as a Graham-style value investor in today's market is limited, and here's why: back then, Graham could quite easily and confidently calculate the liquidation value of a steel manufacturer's inventory, machinery and equipment based on readily available market prices, as one key input to determine the worth of that company. From there, he would invest in that steel manufacturer if say, its market capitalization exceeded its net current asset value (current assets minus total liabilities). But how do you calculate Google's worth when intangible assets make up the majority of its business? Think about it; the value of intangible assets (e.g. technology) is not terminal and can be transitory because that value often does not stand the test of time from the effects of innovation or competition.

The proliferation of information (internet), combined with more professionals working in the finance industry has also largely limited opportunities for so-called value investors. In other words, if a stock is cheap, it is probably cheap for a reason and not because other investors don't understand the "real" value of the company – because now anyone can access that information. I'll cringe if I see investors buy a stock just because it has suffered a big decline from its previous high.

Benjamin Graham, later in his career, admitted, "I am no longer an advocate of elaborate techniques of security analysis in order to find superior value opportunities. This was a rewarding activity, say, 40 years ago, when our textbook Graham and Dodd was first published, but the situation has changed a great deal since then."

In my opinion, the choice between growth investing and value investing can be decided on by answering one question: do you want to invest in the best, and up-and-coming companies, injecting them with capital to grow, and generating 20% + compound annual returns over the long run? Or would you rather invest in 'has-been' companies, that can maybe generate one-off 10-100% returns if their stock prices revert back to "fair value"? Amazon vs. Sears. Apple vs. Nokia. Netflix vs. Blockbuster. I think the answer is clear; growth investing is the way to go.

CHAPTER 3

MY 72 RULES FOR INVESTING IN STOCKS

Now that you know more about growth investing from the previous chapter, and what it means to be a growth investor, I will share my thoughts on the market, including which types of stocks I pick, and why, so that you can get into my head. I feel that I can share all of this knowledge with you now because of everything I have learned, and experienced in the stock market over the past 13 years. It hasn't been an easy ride; that's for sure.

I was invested in the market through the financial crisis ('08), two bear markets (2011 and 2015), and a handful of corrections over my 13-year DIY-investing journey. There were lots of ups and downs, and memorable moments. So, while it's not all perfectly structured, containing lots of rough notes, I've packed in as many lessons as possible for you in "My 72 Rules on Investing in Stocks". I don't hold back. Some readers might take offense at what I say in certain parts, but it's all the cold hard truth based on the many thing's I've learned the hard way. Honestly, I wish I knew all of these lessons 13 years ago. It frustrates me at times thinking how much more money I could have made in the stock market. Growing pains.

For the budding investor, these 72 Rules will hopefully help get you started in the stock market. But for the experienced investor; maybe there's something new here that you didn't think about before, or at least that my rules validate how you have been investing in the market for all these years. By the way, I arbitrarily chose 72 Rules (it was originally 70) because of the "Rule of 72", where one can divide 72 by their investment return (e.g. 15%) to determine how many years it would take for their money to double. A 15% compound annual return is the magical number for me, which means my portfolio would double every 4.8 years. That's my goal.

My 72 Rules on Investing in Stocks:

1. I only hold 25-50 core stocks in my portfolio, because at that point I'm well-diversified, and am not diluting my portfolio with 'so-so' picks. I have high conviction in my current holdings. Plus, I can more easily follow 25-50 stocks on a quarterly basis than I can 50+ stocks. Any number above 50 stocks and it becomes a circus to manage my portfolio, and my efforts to diversify turns into "diworsification". Naturally, the number of holdings in my portfolio increases as I start to find, and invest in new opportunities. Certain points in the market cycle present me with more opportunities (e.g. new technology, de-regulation, IPOs, spin-offs, etc.)

2. I don't let any stock grow larger than 10% of my portfolio. That opens me up to potential risk (if one large holding blows up). My winners will approach 10% position size as they grow, so I take profit off the table, and allocate that capital to new emerging growth opportunities. Position size, and how much money you allocate to high, medium, and low conviction holdings becomes very important as your portfolio grows.

3. I only invest in companies in which I can confidently project future cash flows. I can't confidently project cash flows for companies in cyclical industries like mining, oil & gas, resources, financial services, or pharmaceuticals, etc. I lost a lot of money on Lundin Mining in 2007 / 2008 (-85%), and learned my lesson. Now I avoid the mining sector like the plague. It's extremely rare for investors to actually make money in cyclical industries, and if they do – it's short-lived, and by nature – cyclical. Robert Hirschberg, a family friend, parlayed $20k into $15 million speculating in junior mining stocks. You can find a video online featuring Robert where he tells his story. Also, in a *Globe and Mail* ("Me and My Money" column), Robert explained the four things that he looks for in a junior mining company: 1) executives with successful track records building up junior companies; 2) good assets; 3) access to funding; and 4) lots of upside ("blue sky potential"). So, you can certainly try to invest in cyclical industries, but it's tough! Seriously – even smart people fail. I find it funny when I see complex excel models that project 10 years of cash flow in unpredictable businesses. That's like putting lipstick on a pig, and an ill-fated attempt at fortune-telling, especially when past earnings, or cash flow haven't even been consistent, like 10% growth in year 1, 50% in year 2, and -2% in year 3. Cash flow and earnings like that are extremely volatile, and volatility disables my ability to project the path of future profitability in a company.

4. Similarly, I don't invest in "price-takers", like oil & gas companies that have to price what they sell based on prevailing crude oil market prices. For example, before the recent oil crash (2014–2015), oil producers could pump oil out of the ground and then sell it for $110, which was the prevailing crude oil market price at that time. But then after the oil crash, those same oil producers sold that oil for $30 – a loss since their costs to extract oil were now higher than the price at which they sold oil. Instead, I invest in "price-setters"; companies that can independently raise prices year-after-year to generate higher revenues, and profits for their shareholders.

5. There's only two ways a company can continually increase revenue over time: by raising prices or increasing volume, whether that's through increasing the number of customers, average transaction size, or transactions per customer. I invest in companies that can achieve both price and volume growth. I like focusing on revenue because it's virtually impossible to fudge top-line revenue figures through financial engineering, like it can be done with net income / profit, and especially EBITDA, which I've heard jokingly called "Earnings Before I Tricked the Dumb Auditors". Revenue needs to be sustainable and recurring over time. I don't like lumpy, and inconsistent 'one-off' revenue. I find it amazing that a 'dollar' store – Dollarama – can consistently increase its store count (volume) and its prices (higher than a dollar!) over time like clockwork. That's why I'm a happy Dollarama shareholder.

6. I really like companies that can expand globally.

Think about a company's products / services' addressable market. The growth potential is enormous when the addressable market is possibly everyone in the world – think Facebook. That's why companies that can become near-monopolies with little-to-no competition are ideal investments, especially at early stages in their business life cycle. Peter Thiel's book, *Zero to One*, is a great read on how some companies can go from a niche idea to a monopoly – grab the book from your local library. Thiel's a smart guy. He made a $500,000 investment in Facebook before most people even signed up to the social networking website.

7. The companies that I invest in need to have a competitive advantage, whether that's through their operating model, distribution network, brands, niche products / services, patents, technology, regulatory protection, goodwill, or whatever else that sets them apart. I ask myself , "How hard would it be for a competitor to steal any of their business?" And, "Can technology or innovation disrupt this company's business model?" I also use Porter's Five Forces to validate a company's competitive advantage. Porter's Five Forces can be analyzed for any weaknesses as shown here:

- Threat of new entrants;
- Threat of substitutes;
- Bargaining power of customers;
- Bargaining power of suppliers;
- Industry rivalry

Also, one should study Morningstar's Five (5) Sources of an Economic Moat (in a Company):

- Intangible Assets
- Switching Costs
- Network Effect
- Cost Advantage
- Efficient Scale

Some sources of moats are better than others. Morningstar's Paul Larson explained in an interview on Morningstar.com that "what we found is companies that benefit from intangible assets actually have the best returns on capital by a fairly wide margin relative to the other sources of moat. Conversely, the source of moat that has the lowest fundamental performance [is found within] the efficient-scale companies, and this makes sense if you think about it intuitively. The efficient-scale dynamic is based on companies having an attractive niche that they have positive economic profits, that they have a moat, but not so profitable and so attractive that they are going to attract new competition into the market. So, it makes sense that the efficient-scale companies would have the lowest returns on capital."

But the missing element in the competitive advantage examples above is continual innovation. "If your only defense against invading armies is a moat, you will not last long," Tesla's CEO, Elon Musk said. "What matters is the pace of innovation — that is the fundamental determinant of competitiveness." It's true – the companies you invest in must always be innovating – essentially, aggressively competing with *themselves*, otherwise another competitor will outcompete them.

8. Cost cutting isn't a business strategy. Companies that cost-cut to generate profit, and appease the 'street' (Wall Street, Bay Street...) for however long aren't worth my time or money. You can only cut costs so much until there's really nothing great that remains of a company. I want revenue growth. Companies that are growing are hiring, investing, and spending (e.g. Shopify announcing their $500M investment into a new Toronto office – 2018).

9. I don't invest in any old-economy industries or businesses that are going bust in the future. Newspapers, anyone? This seems obvious but it's a classic value trap; 'cheap' that gets cheaper, and cheaper, and cheaper. The best case study is the Blockbuster-to-Netflix wealth transfer. Why would anyone have invested in Blockbuster near its final bottom? Because they thought it was cheap, and would bounce back. I always invest in relatively new businesses and avoid mature business models. I want to invest in the wealth-recipients, like Netflix in this example. Thomas Rowe Price Jr., who some call "the father of growth investing", said that "it is better to be early than too late in recognizing the passing of one era, the waning of old investment favorites and the advent of a new era affording new opportunities for the investor." But even worse than being too late, is completely and stubbornly betting against the advent of a new era, like one U.S. Hedge Fund Manager who interestingly in 2018 was still shorting Amazon, Netflix, and Tesla – his so-called "bubble-basket" of emerging companies, contributing to severe underperformance in 2018 throughout a very broad bull market. Short sellers who get it wrong; collectively shorting a large percentage of a company's float, can inadvertently cause a short squeeze, which happens when they capitulate, covering their shorts after a company announces positive earnings, among other positive catalysts, thus causing the stock to shoot much higher. Sometimes investing in heavily shorted companies with a lot of future growth can lead to big gains, especially when they're still small companies, like *The Trade Desk (TTD)* in 2018 for example.

10. Companies should be earning high rates of return on capital (ROIC), generally around 15%, and at a minimum above their cost of capital consistently over the last 5 years but preferably over the last 10 years, e.g. 15%, 16%, 15%, 16%, 15%, 16%, 15%, 16%, 15%, 16% ROIC. I don't rely on Return on Equity (ROE) as a measure as it can be distorted with big debt loads, and lots of debt as a percentage of book value or market capitalization can sink companies. Though, for smaller companies, ROIC is not a determining factor for investment. Small companies are still focusing on growth, and so what matters is their future cash flows, and present revenue growth. Remember, the present value of a company is the total of all its future cash flows discounted back to today.

11. What happens at the company level needs to also happen at the per share level. For example, growth in net income translating into an increase in earnings per share (EPS). It's all about you; the shareholder. Some management continually dilute their existing shareholders through mass expansion of shares, in other words; using their shares carelessly as currency. I don't like that. So, look for growth in earnings per share (EPS), book value per share, and free cash flow per share over time, and only accept anomalies if there's a real excuse or if the company is small. As said before; focus on a small company's revenue growth, future cash flow, and its path to profitability in the next 1-5 years. In the long run, though, you'll make money in stocks from two things: one is earnings growth and then the other is what multiple investors ultimately pay for that earnings growth.

12. I focus my stock picks in the more inefficient small-cap and mid-cap segments of the market. Those are the smaller-market-capitalization companies ($100 million to $10 billion in size) that can double, triple, quadruple, and more. If I owned mostly large cap companies ($10 - $150 billion+), I would probably just be replicating the index (e.g. S&P 500, DJIA, TSX/60) and its performance. I want to beat the index. Now that I have a solid foundation of small-cap and mid-cap companies in my portfolio, I've been investing in micro-caps (< $100M market cap), which are often perceived to be more risky, but can lead to incredibly outsized returns if one picks the right stocks. 100-baggers are my goal. You'll learn more about micro-caps in the chapter, *Small Companies; Big Dreams*.

13. When there's a systemic market decline; recession (e.g. financial crisis '08), bear market (e.g. TSX 2015), or the common correction, which happens more than you think, I'll invest lots more money into my existing stock holdings. Remember, the world isn't *actually* going to end when the stock market goes down. The problem that some investors have is that they're always waiting for the next BIG pull-back (-50% declines). Most of these investors lived through the financial crisis, and / or the technology boom and bust, and so they remain on the sidelines, and expect to buy great companies cheap right now, and all the time. It isn't that easy. I'll continue to buy great companies on the way up. But don't get me wrong, when a systemic crash does happen, I'll happily buy more into great growth companies at cheaper prices. Here's some tips on investing during a stock market crash and / or economic recession:

- Buy stocks on sale. When a recession hits, investors pull out of the stock market. This leaves you the opportunity to pick quality stocks on sale.

- Ignore the media. The newspaper industry sells more newspapers with negative headline news. Naturally, the media will pump fear into you. Ignore that fear, and invest in stocks.

- Remember, the economy will bounce back. Have you ever been sick and thought you would never get better? That is how people think during a recession.

- Even if the stock market keeps on tanking after you invest, the underlying businesses may still be in growth mode – buy the future cash flows.

- If you cannot stomach a -50% loss or more, do not invest in the stock market. At the nadir of the financial crisis – March 2009 – my stock portfolio was down close-to-50% (ouch!). But I fought back my fear and invested more.

- The stock market will reach its nadir (within a recession) once all unemployment, bankruptcy, and earnings figures are the worst that can be reported, because the market is forward-looking. So when the media shifts its focus, the market is likely already rebounding, making new highs.

- If you invest when there's 'blood on the street',

invest big. You will be kicking yourself if you buy one share in Company A when a year after the recession, Company A's stock return is +200%.

- Invest when people are fully depressed about the economy or stock market and when investor participation is low. Remember; the stock market transfers wealth from the impatient to the patient. You know you are too late to the recovery when analysts start slapping buy ratings on every stock.

I like systemic stock market crashes because I can buy great companies at cheaper prices when everything goes down. But when an individual stock drops in price, among a normal range-bound market, I think long and hard before investing more money in that company (dollar cost averaging), because...

14. Managing a portfolio is like gardening. I water the flowers and pull the weeds. I like a big, beautiful garden. In other words, I reward my existing holdings (the "winners") by increasing my stake in them if and when they post great earnings results quarter after quarter. I like to see 20-25%+ EPS growth, but also anything higher, realizing that that kind of parabolic growth can't last forever. I recently read an article in the Forbes's 100th Anniversary Edition that revealed an exchange between Peter Lynch and Warren Buffett on this garden analogy:

Peter Lynch: "I got a call from Warren Buffett in 1989. My daughter picks up the phone and says, 'It's Mr. Buffett on the line.' And I thought some of my buddies are kidding me because she was only 6. And I pick up the phone, and I hear, 'This is Warren Buffett from Omaha, Nebraska.' You know, he talks so fast. 'And I love your book, One Up on

Wall Street, and I want to use a line from it in my year-end report. I have to have it. Can I please use it?' I said, 'Sure. What's the line?' He says, 'Selling your winners and holding your losers is like cutting the flowers and watering the weeds.'"

15. Underperforming cheap stocks (those "weeds"), can get cheaper, and cheaper, and cheaper, and when they do, you'll understand that they were originally cheap for a reason. That's called a "value trap". I've probably said this already, but it's worth repeating; not all stocks bounce back as some investors hope (and pray!). There's a famous picture of hedge fund manager, Paul Tudor Jones relaxing in his office with his feet kicked up. A single sheet of paper is tacked on the wall behind him with a phrase written out in black marker: "Losers Average Losers" – as known as dollar cost averaging (buying a stock continually as it drops in price, just because it's getting perceivably cheaper).

Take a look at Citigroup; it went from $550/share (2007) to $25/share (2009) as a result of the financial crisis, and is still only at $70/share now (2018). That's a terrible crash, and paltry "rebound" if you can even call it that as Citigroup is nowhere near its $550/share high. It really pains me to watch investors try to catch a falling knife, thinking it's a so-called "value stock", and then letting that eventual 'has-been' stock sit in their portfolios. That dead money could be invested in better companies ("opportunity cost"). I am always happy to pay a little more to invest in quality growth stocks because I'm buying a company's future cash flows, not just what it's worth today, and especially not what it was worth in the past.

16. The companies that I invest in don't have a lot of

long term debt on their balance sheets. Preferably, no debt at all because it's virtually impossible for a company to go bankrupt if it doesn't have any debt. Overall, I prefer tightly controlled and clean balance sheets, and take into consideration a business' current ratio, as well as its debt / equity ratio. Always demand good balance sheets – think of it as a company's "net worth".

17. Free cash flow is king. Companies that generate high amounts of free cash flow, combined with exceptional capital allocation, can grow at high rates of return through reinvestment back into their business, smart acquisitions, and opportune share buybacks if shares are cancelled over a prolonged period of time. Plus, lots of cash means companies can self-fund their business, not having to heavily rely on the debt or equity markets, and even thrive throughout economic down-cycles when credit dries up. In contrast; the resource boom, which mushroomed in Canada from 2000 to 2007. It was a period where many junior mining IPO's emerged on the stock market. Once the financial crisis hit in 2007, those junior mining shareholders watched helplessly as capital (in the form of loans) shriveled up as banks tightened their lending practices and existing loan books in order to shore up capital. Exceptional free cash flow generators are those companies that require less capital expenditure to run their business – definitely not mining companies. High capital expenditure intense companies are sluggish, requiring too much capital to grow, and even then deliver low returns, and not much lasting shareholder value. I'll pass. Capital-light businesses are for me. Think Software-as-a-Service (SaaS), among other more effective, and efficient business models.

18. The free cash flow / enterprise value ratio (FCF/EV) might be one of the best, but overlooked metrics one can use to identify exceptional and inefficiently priced Capital Compounder stocks. The higher the percentage figure the better. That combined with high return on capital (ROIC) to demonstrate effective allocation of free cash flow.

19. Buy and hold "forever" doesn't actually work. Sure, Warren Buffett says that his favourite holding period is "forever", but his wish doesn't always come true. Recent case in point; Buffett's investment in IBM (2017), which he unloaded fairly quickly. I have come to understand and accept that businesses don't last forever. As Chuck Palahniuk wrote in the fantastic book (and movie adaptation), Fight Club: "On a long enough time line, the survival rate for everyone [including businesses] drops to zero." It is basic high school business class curriculum, where we learned companies go through linear, and almost pre-destined stages: Seed, Start-up, Growth, Established, Expansion, Mature, and then Exit. Look at the Dow Jones, S&P 500, and other major indexes throughout history. Companies are listed and de-listed over time. Exxon Mobil was the king (i.e., highest market cap) in 2009. Apple is the king in 2018. Things change. Change is constant. So, I make money when and where I can, from "Start-up" to "Growth" through "Expansion", and don't hold onto a dying company past its maturity date, because that's like drinking spoiled milk.

20. I always strive to maintain around a 15% compound annual return in my portfolio. If one of my stock holdings isn't keeping up with the pace, I'll sell and allocate that money into a company that can generate higher returns. Only exception is my micro-cap stocks, which are more volatile by nature (thinly traded, less institutional ownership, and low-to-no analyst coverage). I'm always thinking about opportunity cost; where money can work the hardest for me at any given time. Generally, a company's compound returns are correlated to its return on capital (ROIC) over the long run. That's why the stock holdings in my portfolio average 15% to 20% Return on Capital; because I want to achieve a 15% compound annual return. Though it's important to note that a higher than average ROIC is generally not sustainable in the long-run.

21. I never invest in stocks *just because* they have high dividend yields. Most of my holdings have low or no dividend yields, because capital is used in more effective ways (e.g. re-investment back into the business). High dividend yields are indicative of large-caps, mature businesses, and naturally in some cases – businesses in decline. In the latter case, companies that slash dividends send their stock prices into further decline, especially if those stocks were labelled as "high-yielders", and largely owned by senior citizens seeking a "retirement package portfolio", or institutional investors with a high yield fund mandate. If you want safe yield; buy a bond or GIC – but even then I don't recommend it.

22. I buy into "growth at a reasonable price" or "GARP", meaning that I won't invest in a stock with a 25 P/E and 10% EPS growth rate, but will happily buy a stock with a 30 P/E and 30%+ EPS growth rate. It's all about the future growth. But try telling that to a value investor. For many investors, the famous P/E (price to earnings) indicator is the first, and sometimes only indicator that is referenced to glean a stock's valuation. However, P/E, which is calculated by dividing a stock's price by its current earnings, is a lagging indicator. Why? P/E only accounts for the current valuation of a stock. It does not take into account the future potential in a stock's growth, and thus doesn't accurately judge its valuation. This is why I like to use the forward P/E to valuate a stock, as it takes into account future earnings. Forward P/E is calculated by dividing a stock's price by its forecasted earnings (next year's estimated earnings). Imagine passing up on a stock because you decide that 20 P/E is too high, while, unbeknownst to you, the forward P/E is 11 because of high earnings forecasts that are likely to materialize (if it's in a predictable, non-cyclical industry), supported by the company's management team in their forward guidance estimates.

23. I don't buy obscure "net-nets" (companies where their current assets minus total liabilities is lower than its market capitalization), or in other words, "*deep* value" stocks that I know nothing about, hoping that the market will see what I see and then finally bid the price of the stock back up to its underlying net-asset value. That could take months, years…never. "Net-nets" aren't worth your money. Sorry, Benjamin Graham.

24. I need to really understand each of the businesses in my portfolio, and my specific reason for owning them. That means all of my stocks (80% +) fall into these 3 industries: consumer franchise, technology, and diversified industries (e.g. Savaria – assisted living). Some people want to look smart by investing into complex, and ever-changing industries like bio-technology, but I like boring, and unglamorous companies that generate high return on capital on a consistent basis. Bonus points if they're leaders in their respective industries. Some of my best investments of all time are in companies that I spotted in the mall, supermarket, and out and about; the products and services that people buy on a recurring basis. You should do the same. I don't invest in the stock market to look, or sound smart – I do it to make money, and so I buy what I know. Along these lines, I don't shy away from buying great companies in the "female-space", like Estee Lauder, which owns MAC Cosmetics, among other profitable assets. Because the investment industry consists mainly of men, I can have an informational advantage in stocks that they might not want to touch for whatever reason – these stocks don't have "cooties"!

25. Before I initiate a new position, I don't first think, "How much money can I make?" Instead, I ask myself, "How much money can I lose?" I consider all the ways a stock can lose money before I even think about the upside.

26. I accept that I'll have losers in my DIY investing journey; some stocks will decline, and not work out. But it's my job to make sure that my winners always outnumber and outperform my losers. I just have to swallow my pride. Investing can be a probability game even after countless hours of fundamental research into each stock, and after many years of investing in the stock market. As I progress through my journey, my losers aren't as much a result of investing in companies outside of my circle of competence (e.g. biotech), as they are placing too much faith in management that doesn't execute on its vision and growth projections, or it's the result of misjudging the business model, products and services. But that's life – you can't win them all.

27. The stock market has buyers and sellers. I want to make sure that when it's time to sell my stocks in the future, that there's buyers who want to purchase from me. This "high-level", simplistic thinking has saved me from making bad investments that nobody wants to buy back from me in the future. Similarly, I don't want to be the "greater-fool" or last "bag holder"; investing in a mature / declining business at the peak of its cycle, taking it off the hands of the smarter investor who's now selling out of his position. The "greater fool theory", which Burton Malkiel alludes to throughout his book, *A Random Walk Down Wall Street*, states that the "price of an object is determined not by its intrinsic value, but rather by irrational beliefs and expectations of market participants. A price can be justified by a rational buyer under the belief that another party is willing to pay an even higher price. In other words, one may pay a price that seems 'foolishly' high because one may rationally have the expectation that the item can be resold to a 'greater fool' later". I want to invest in a start-up company, or a company that has just entered its growth phase, where it's worked out the kinks in its business model and simply needs to replicate its successful formula until it can't anymore.

28. The majority of my bigger, core positions are in mid-cap companies that continually earn high return on capital (ROIC), generate free cash flow, and grow their earnings and book value per share through the expansion phase in their business cycle. But I'll also plant seeds in smaller companies that have yet to fully prove themselves, let alone generate a profit (net income). My mantra is to plant seeds and water the trees. Here's a story: I attended the Toronto Money Show in 2017, and to my surprise, Gordon Pape's presentation was by far my favourite. Why? Because I thought Pape was only going to discuss large-cap, safe, 'steady-eddy' stocks. Pape's a wise, old man (he's 82), with many years of experience in the market. Nevertheless, he talked about Shopify; it was one of his top picks. I was surprised because Pape had invested through lots of market cycles (ups and downs) since 1957 (~ 60 years), and through the technology boom and bust in 2000. So, he's seen speculative, outright bad technology stocks (e.g. TheGlobe.com, eToys.com, Pets.com, and Webvan) during his time, and yet Pape liked Shopify (which I also own in my portfolio), investing in it around its IPO, even though it wasn't (and still isn't) generating a profit. Seems he likes startup companies too.

I'll invest more money as my seed companies' plans do play out, but to hedge a bet in a very small company, I'll ask myself, "Is this company an acquisition target; does it have assets that a much larger company would want?". Sometimes the returns from small-caps, especially those with a very short public life, are mostly a result of it getting bought-out by a much larger company. Also, when I invest in small companies, there should be as much 'optionality' as possible (e.g. takeover potential, among other factors). When I interviewed Martin Braun for *Market Masters*, he shared his thoughts on optionality:

"Optionality is a buzzword for 'pregnant with possibility.' It's a fancy way of saying 'upside.' So there's a

lot of cheap optionality embedded in stocks. In other words, you're not paying for this happening, and you're not paying for that happening; you're paying maybe a little teeny bit for a third thing and maybe a little bit more for a fourth thing happening to the stock. If any of those four things were to happen you'd make good money because the market's not really paying for them. Any one of them. But if all four of them kicked in, oh my god! That's what I mean by optionality. The optionality is the part of the equation that the market has not paid for. What the market has already paid for is the risk; the disappointment the market might face when it realizes that what it's been paying for isn't going to happen. They were thinking that the company was going to make a dollar a share and it only made 90 cents. They say, 'Oh, I'm so disappointed,' and the stock goes down. Because the market was paying for a dollar. But if the market was paying for 75 cents and the company makes 90 cents, then, 'Oh, the market's happy,' and the stock goes up. What you have to worry about is what the market expects and what it is paying for. Will it come short or not? If it does miss, then maybe I lose 10% and if you can live with that, then that's the downside. But what about all the good things that could happen? Other than that possible 10% hit, you're getting it for free."

I counted on both hands all of the optionality before investing in a marijuana company called Tweed at $1.50/share in 2015. That 'seed' turned into a pretty big 'tree', now called Canopy Growth Corp.

I'll cover lots of examples of optionality (or "catalysts") in a later chapter, but here I'll share my friend's two clever ways to comfortably invest in small companies, in which he respectively calls "Remora" and "Breaching Water":

Remora Strategy – (It's that sucker fish that rides sharks and feeds off its scraps) – companies that benefit from another larger company's growth. Examples would be Tucows that provides domain names to Shopify, or Pacific Insights [since bough-out] that benefitted from Tesla car sales growth. The "remora" company is normally not as well-known and trades on a cheaper relative price. Notice that Tesla and Shopify don't have profitable bottom lines; Pacific Insights and Pacific Insights do, however.

Breaching Water Strategy – Companies that are just on the cusp of hitting profitability. Once profitable, this will attract investors. You can sometimes chart the profit and expense lines and find the likely date profitability will occur. To find these, more work is needed and it may require playing with a financial model to identify when this event will occur. Examples under this strategy would include XPO logistics, and Greenspace Brands.

29. I never *really* want to lose 50% on any stock. It's important for me to know when to cut my losses before I lose too much capital, because a 50% loss requires a 100% gain to revert back-to-even, and then getting-back-to-even is exponentially harder the more money one loses. However, I understand that smaller companies are more volatile than larger ones, and so I give the micro caps more slack. I'm not so nice with my mid-cap stocks though. I don't want to dig myself into a hole and then struggle to get back out. Life's too short for that.

30. I'm wary of "blue chips". Unlike conventional wisdom, they're never a sure-thing in the stock market. I can list lots of once "blue chip" companies that don't exist today or are shells of once larger companies (e.g. Research in Motion – RIM / BlackBerry). Blue chips are not as "defensive" as one would think. Mature businesses are ripe for disruption. One day after work (this was 2006, and I was 19), I was riding the go-train home (Lakeshore West), and started talking with the train's onboard ambassador – the guy who announces the stops on the intercom. After some small-talk, and upon him learning that I had just started investing in the stock market, he told me, "Son (he was around 65), I've done really well in Citigroup, Bank of America, and Yellow Pages. Buy blue chip stocks that pay a dividend, and you'll do just fine...." Well, I didn't buy any of those so called "blue chips" in 2006, which all subsequently crashed, never to really return again. Thank goodness! Another "blue-chip" – Nortel Networks. On a plane trip from Toronto to Vancouver in 2002, I overheard an Air Canada flight attendant talking with one of the passengers about his dreadful investment in Nortel, which during the technology boom was *the* market darling in Canada. Interestingly, about half the passengers on the plane turned their heads, indicating to me that they too lost lots of money in Nortel. The morale here is that whenever a stock is too good to be true – even if it's labelled a "blue-chip" and everyone owns the stock – it probably isn't that great and you'll likely be disappointed. I like to find companies that are undiscovered, and under the radar. I don't just buy stocks because others buy them – that's what sheep do (if they could trade stocks).

31. I would get a bit anxious if and when normal-average-everyday people, who've never bought stocks in their lives, enter the stock market because of a certain hot sector, hot stock, or convincing broker. Especially when they start saying, "it can only go up" and "it's so easy to make money right now", without conducting any fundamental research on the companies in their portfolios. Watch Seinfeld's "The Stock Tip", Season One, Episode 5 for an entertaining take on this phenomena. When everyone enters the market is probably a good sign that a peak is forming (e.g. Cryptocurrencies in late 2017). There's that great story from Joseph Kennedy where he said that when the shoe-shine boy or the cabbie started to give him investment advice, he knew that it was time to sell or short everything. But I also realize that markets can stay euphoric for far longer than one thinks, which is why I never cash out of the market. I stick with great companies as long as they're great, growing, and generating wealth for me – the shareholder. I don't just sell when I think my stocks have become "overvalued" (unless any have crossed my 10% portfolio size threshold; in which case I'll trim), or when the market is reaching its "peak", based on what some so-called "expert" on TV says. On the other hand, some people might never buy stocks because they're always "too expensive", and then they miss out on every market bull rally until they die. Now that would be sad. As Martin Zweig said: "One of the frustrating things for people who miss the first rally in a bull market is that they wait for the big correction, and it never comes. The market just keeps climbing and climbing."

32. I accept that I'm not going to get rich quick, even though I'd like to be on the beach right now, sipping on a rum n' coke. I control any feelings of greed because greed can lead to very stupid decisions in the stock market, including, but not limited to a terrible case of "FOMO" – Fear of Missing Out. FOMO can make even the most astute investors want to buy the worst stocks, just because they're going up at an astronomical rate. But I don't feel 'smart' when my stocks have gone up in a bull market because a rising tide lifts all boats, and so that means I definitely don't speculate. Conversely, I invest more in the market when I feel fearful, because that's when most people are selling stocks, and driving down stock prices so that they're cheaper for more patient investors. As Jesse Livermore, pinnacle character of the famous book, *Reminiscences of a Stock Operator*, said: "All through time, people have basically acted and reacted the same way in the market as a result of: greed, fear, ignorance, and hope. That is why the numerical formations and patterns recur on a constant basis. What has happened in the past will happen again, and again, and again". To put this into perspective, over the past 80 years, an investment in Canadian stocks has grown 1,597-fold despite 13 recessions, double-digit interest rates, and several world crises. Same goes for the American markets. Following each downturn, stocks have gone on to reach new highs, while many investors remained scared out of their minds.

33. I research micro-cap, small-cap and mid-cap companies as much as possible. It's a daily routine, one in which you'll read more about in a later chapter. I can truly have an informational edge in these overlooked smaller companies, with little-to-no institutional ownership or analyst coverage. Conversely, for the most part everything is already priced into those liquid, well-known large cap companies like Verizon, or Bell. There's no opportunity for me to generate "alpha" there; in other words, beat the market. That's why when certain events (catalysts) effect small companies, you'll often times see a big boost in the price of the stock once that new information gets "priced in", as there were no expectations leading up to the event. Remember; very small companies usually have no analyst coverage). Some of these key catalysts that move small stocks are as follows:

- New (big) accounts
- New bolt-on products / services
- New verticals
- New geographies;
- Accretive acquisitions
- Exit (i.e. takeover by larger company)

34. I don't care about any macro-economic trends. Some people follow the Federal Reserve (U.S.) or Central Bank (Canada), watching and waiting for any change in the overnight rates, but I really don't care. I don't follow macro trends in rates, or the change in money supply, or whatever else that doesn't really matter at all to the companies in my portfolio. I just invest in great non-cyclical companies that sell products in good times and in bad times.

35. When I pull up a company's metrics on a 10-year table (I use Morningstar.com), I'll know in under one minute if I've found something special when the business is growing at a consistently high rate over time, and especially if it's posted little-to-no downside during a recession. That's important; I always check to see how a business performs through a recession. Bonus points!

36. A company's stock price performance matches its

underlying business' growth overtime. My favourite companies have stock charts that rise steadily, in line with their intrinsic growth, and with very low volatility in their stock prices. Just an almost perfect upward trend line. These stocks are difficult to find in the market (which is why I call this a 'treasure hunt'). But Lassonde Industries comes to mind and is a good illustration. Lassonde Industries is endowed with a strong brand portfolio of 2nd-tier juice brands: Allen's, Everfresh, Fairlee, Fruite, Oasis, Rougemont, Sunlike, and Tropical Grove. I initially invested in Lassonde Industries when it was trading at an incredibly low Price-to-Sales (P/S) of 0.55 in 2008, and have held the stock since – it's part of my list of 40 "Capital Compounders".

37. When I first learn about a new company, I add it to my watchlist, conduct further research, and follow it for some time before I decide to initiate a positon. I give myself a cool-off period to avoid buying any stocks on emotion. This is especially important when investing in emerging new industries, for example; 3-D printing. One needs to have a "wait and see" approach when investing in extremely early-stage industries. But use common sense. For example, people often assume that Marijuana is a *new* industry – but it's not! Automobiles, though, were a new, emerging industry, and so it would have been tough to place bets. During the early-to-mid 1900's, hundreds of automobile companies were founded in America, but only three companies survived: Ford, GM, and Chrysler. So, in an emerging industry, wait (but don't wait too long) until you can more confidently predict the future market leader(s). Understand "survivorship bias", which is the error of concentrating on the stocks that make it past some selection process and overlooking those that did not, typically because of their lack of visibility. To illustrate, I'll use Peter Thiel as an example. He's the guy who invested around $500,000 in Facebook when Zuckerberg was still super-young, and before anyone really knew about the company. Thiel's a billionaire now but we only heard about Thiel as a result of his investment in Facebook, which could've been a failure. We don't hear about the investors who invested in Friendster, or the companies like Friendster that didn't make it. The lesson here is that successful investing is ultimately a combination of foresight, luck, and risk. For every one billionaire, there's thousands who also tried to make it there. For every unicorn ($1 Billion valuation company), there's thousands of companies that tried, and failed. I just do as much as possible to increase my odds of winning, and that means spreading bets like a Venture Capitalist would – it's that one, or two, or three companies that you invest in out of hundreds that will thrust your portfolio's value upwards. I'm talking 30x, 40x, 50x returns. But that's not to say you should indiscriminately spread bets, because...

38. Only 10% of the Canadian stock market is investable in my opinion, with ~ 50 truly exceptional businesses at any given time. So you must do your research, and limit your universe to the *best* stocks. I find that there's something special about Quebec, a province in which many great companies are born, and operate. Perhaps it's because the Caisse de dépôt et placement du Québec takes fairly substantial positions in the underwriting for Quebec companies to help them grow and expand worldwide into new markets. Many of the most successful stocks in my portfolio, based on annual rates of return, are Quebec-based companies: Alimentation Couche-Tard, Dollarama, Canadian National Railway, CGI, Lassonde Industries, TFI International, CAE, Gildan Activewear, MTY Food Group, Richelieu Hardware, Saputo, Stella-Jones and Savaria, to name just a few. Perhaps it's that not only do Quebec companies benefit from the Caisse de dépôt's financial support, but they also have some of the best and most shareholder-friendly management teams in Canada. Quebec's company landscape is incredibly well diversified, somewhat like the U.S.'s market, and a stark contrast to the broader Canadian market, where there's mostly oil & gas, mining, and financial services companies trading on the TSX. On a purely numbers basis, there's more exceptional companies in the U.S. than in Canada, as the U.S. is around 10x larger, but I would still only say 10% are superior investments at any given time. Keep your universe small.

39. I get excited when I find a great company that issues black and white annual shareholder reports (without photos), has an outdated and amateur logo, and is still using a website that was designed in the early-to-mid 2000s. These are the 'gems' that have yet to be fully discovered by institutions and retail investors – they're still small. Once companies get bigger on the foundation of their success, they upgrade all of those things – shareholder reports, websites, and logos – through big, expensive Marketing, and PR Departments. Examples: Constellation Software's website, or Berkshire Hathaway's website (which still hasn't changed even though it's a huge company.

40. It is usually best when management has a stake in

the company and/or is an owner/operator. Because they're shareholders too, and therefore want the stock price to go up as much as you do. If you've seen Wall Street, you'll vividly remember the scene where Gordon Gekko so eloquently criticizes management in his famous Teldar Paper speech:

"... in the days of the free market, when our country was a top industrial power, there was accountability to the stockholder. The Carnegies, the Mellons, the men that built this great industrial empire, made sure of it because it was their money at stake. Today, management has no stake in the company! All together, these men sitting up here [Teldar management] own less than 3 percent of the company. And where does Mr. Cromwell put his million-dollar salary? Not in Teldar stock; he owns less than 1 percent...".

What better signal of conviction than a manager who owns a part of the very business he manages? With stake in their own business, management is motivated even more to build shareholder value, because they too are shareholders. I honestly don't trust management that doesn't invest their own personal money back into the company. You can find management ("insider") holdings by looking up stocks on insidertracking.com (U.S. market) and canadianinsider.com (Canadian market).

But management must also demonstrate operational excellence, combined with superb capital allocation, intelligence, and a strong drive to compete in the marketplace. Further, management needs to have an achievable vision for the company, with the ability to execute and realize that vision with profitable growth.

Finally, management needs to have integrity. Why integrity? If management is caught with having committed a fraud, or if they break any laws, your investment in a company can quickly go to zero in a week, or in some extreme cases – overnight. If you don't believe me, look into a company called Enron.

Warren Buffett doesn't recommend books often but he did endorse *The Outsiders*, calling it "an outstanding book about CEOs who excelled at capital allocation". *The Outsiders* chronicles eight CEOs whose company's average returns outperformed the S&P 500 by a factor of twenty – in other words, an investment of $10,000 with each of these CEOs, on average, would have been worth over $1.5 million twenty-five years later. *The Outsiders* was a great read. I learned what sets apart the superior CEOs ("Outsiders") from the rest. As an investor, it's important that you understand how to evaluate management, that is the metrics, and indicators that demonstrate a capable CEO. Interestingly, I emailed the author of the book –William N. Thorndike – and asked him which Canadian CEOs in his opinion would fit into the realm of "Outsiders" – CEOs who excel at capital allocation. He replied with one possibility: Bruce Flatt (Brookfield Asset Management), admitting, "I have not done a thorough study of Canada". In the next chapter, I'll share with you who I think are currently Canada's top capital allocators.

41. We're at a point in time where every industry is being disrupted by technology. I recommend that you read, "Why Software is Eating the World", by Marc Andreessen, to understand this reality. It's not just the technology companies anymore, like Apple (iPhone) disrupting RIM

(BlackBerry) in the smartphone business, for example. Every product, service and industry is being disrupted at a faster rate than ever before, which is why I also like to invest in companies that serve a need / want that *can't* easily be disrupted by technology in the next 10 years. Food, and drinks, for example. Everyone will still be eating food, and drinking beverages the same way they do today in 10 years' time. Technology won't change that basic human need and behaviour. But don't just take it from me. Here's what Jeff Bezos, Founder and CEO of Amazon, has to say about the future:

"I very frequently get the question: 'What's going to change in the next 10 years?' And that is a very interesting question; it's a very common one. I almost never get the question: 'What's not going to change in the next 10 years?' And I submit to you that that second question is actually the more important of the two -- because you can build a business strategy around the things that are stable in time. ... [I]n our retail business, we know that customers want low prices, and I know that's going to be true 10 years from now. They want fast delivery; they want vast selection. It's impossible to imagine a future 10 years from now where a customer comes up and says, 'Jeff I love Amazon; I just wish the prices were a little higher,' [or] 'I love Amazon; I just wish you'd deliver a little more slowly.' Impossible. And so the effort we put into those things, spinning those things up, we know the energy we put into it today will still be paying off dividends for our customers 10 years from now. When you have something that you know is true, even over the long term, you can afford to put a lot of energy into it.".

So, while I invest in emerging companies that are changing the world, I also invest in companies that will be around for years to come, and still have growth.

42. If I don't think a stock can become an "x-bagger", I won't invest in the company. A 3-bagger, for example, means that a stock would increase 3 times from its initial purchase price. $100 invested would turn into $300. That's why I like to invest in companies that are under $100 million in market capitalization (micro-caps), and also between $100 million to $10 billion in market capitalization (Small to Mid-Caps). More so on the smaller-end, because if a company makes it, I can potentially earn 100x my investment, and achieve the elusive 100-Bagger. Sure, wishful thinking, and rare, but heck, it could happen! I'll share actual examples of 100-Baggers later in this book.

43. I favour stocks that have strong tailwinds. Some examples include demographics (elder care; Savaria), de-regulation or legalization (marijuana; Canopy Growth Corp), or shifts in consumer taste (sugar reduction, and replacement of diet / aspartame; National Beverage – La Croix). Strong tailwinds drive sales in a select group of companies that are selling those 'beneficiary' products or services to the market. Mark Schmehl, Portfolio Manager with Fidelity Investments Canada, also likes to invest in tailwinds: "Some people try to discover what a stock is worth before they buy... They make the mistake of thinking they can quantify what's unknowable. In my view, if there are tailwinds moving [a stock] forward, it's a 'buy'". For example, Match Group – one of my top ideas for 2018 that I shared in my newsletter at the beginning of the year. Match Group is a consolidator, and operator of popular dating apps; POF, OkCupid, Tinder, and more. Match Group's financials, and growth numbers are very good, and let's face the facts – online dating is now the norm. I was recently talking with my cousin about this shift in dating behaviour, reminiscing that in 2005 maybe 20% of women were on online dating sites and apps. Now 10+ years later, it seems that 80%+ of women are on dating apps, especially Tinder, and the non-Match Group app, Bumble. Guys go to where the women are; that's just how it works. In 2005, most women would say, "dating sites are for losers, and creepers". But now, it's "normal". I will say, though, that even with this shift in dating behavior, I'm still always told, "sorry, I have a boyfriend", when I try to initiate conversations with women on dating apps. Some things never change, eh.

Another example – U.S. Billionaire Mario Gabelli's "Pet Parents" fund (I'm not joking). Pet Parents invests in companies that "generally derive at least 50% of their revenues or profits from... the following sectors: manufacturers and distributors of pet food, pet supplies, veterinary pharmaceuticals, veterinary wellness, veterinary and other pet services, pet equipment, pet toys, and products and services that support Pet Parents regarding their pet activities". Gabelli has seen a strong tailwind in the western world; dogs are now a *woman's* best friend, and women will do (and pay anything) for cute little Max.

44. I don't invest in companies that will just be 'one-hit-wonders'. Growth companies can only maintain their high rates of growth by investing in research and development, expanding their business into new product lines, services, and markets, and evolving with their customers over time.

Innovate or die.

45. As soon as any management blames their problems on external reasons like bad weather (seriously, I've heard this on several quarterly calls... as if customers can't shop online), bad press, and consumer behaviour, among other excuses, I will quickly sell the stock. Management needs to adapt to change and accept their issues before they become BIG problems. I still remember going to RIM's annual shareholder conferences from 2009 – 2011, and listening to both co-CEOs – Lazaridis and Balsillie – trying to convince those in the audience that "people want long lasting batteries, great reception, and keyboards"...

46. I closely watch a company's gross margin over time. Declining gross margins, like in the case of RIM, is a sign that competition is driving down prices. Gross margins started to fall gradually and then rapidly as BlackBerry succumbed to new competition in the smartphone space. BlackBerry's gross margins went from 55% (2006) to 44% (2010) to 35% (2012) to 31% (2013) to -0.6% (2014). While BlackBerry's stock may have seemed cheap at the time by standard valuation measures (P/E), it would turn out to be a value trap due to a collapse in its sales. I only want to invest in businesses that have strong continual pricing power, which is a result of competitive advantage in the marketplace. Tim Hortons (Restaurant Brands International), for example, can probably raise the price of coffee every year from now until eternity and people will still buy a cup of coffee there 2x every day.

47. Even great companies have minor setbacks. But the difficult part is separating the minor setbacks from the big problems. I always sell when there's a big problem that will most likely continually hurt the business going forward. In other words, I sell when my initial thesis to invest in the company is later broken. I don't play 'wait and see'. There's some warning signs that are early "tells" – like the aforementioned decline in gross margins. Some of the other warning signs: CEO / CFO departs company, management delays quarterly earnings report, government or regulatory body opens an investigation into company, revenue / net income declines more-than-normal or is a surprise drop, prominent short seller announces short-position (and reasons for the short), management makes highly-dilutive, and bad acquisition (using shares as currency), large company announces competing product / services, company owner / operator dies, management announces issues with product / service, and / or management cuts the dividend partially or completely. You'll learn about more catalysts (both negative and positive) in a later chapter.

48. Because I invest in more illiquid micro-cap, small-cap and mid-cap stocks, I can stomach volatility. In other words; the ups and down in stock prices, which can mean -25% one day, +10% the next, and so on. But that tolerance to volatility lasts as long as the intrinsic growth trajectory of those companies is going up over time (period of 5+ years). Amazon's stock didn't go straight up. As said before, investors had to have the wherewithal and conviction to withstand the ups and downs of Amazon before they reaped any substantial gains years later. To illustrate, Amazon declined from $95 (1999) to $22/share (2000), losing over 75% of its value in just one year's time. And it would lose 50% of its value in 2008, with similar collapses in between both periods – it was hard to own

Amazon.

49. I mostly focus on Canadian equities, which comprise 80% of my portfolio. I feel that I have an edge because Canada is my home country. I know a lot about the Canadian small-cap, mid-cap, and now more recently, mic-cap companies, all of which you'll find in the chapter on "My Universe of Growth Stocks". Though, 20% of my portfolio is invested in U.S. equities. I was mostly buying U.S. stocks when the Canadian dollar was at-parity and also above-parity at points between 2007 and 2013. I'll buy U.S. stocks with new money again once CAD (vs USD) reaches 90 cents. The only European company that I have invested in is Luxottica, on the basis of their near-monopoly in the sunglasses and prescription glasses space. I generally avoid most publicly traded European and Asian companies (some exceptions are Chinese Technology Companies), as they don't seem to have strong shareholder-oriented management cultures, plus; the North American companies that I invest in sell products and services into those parts of the world.

50. It isn't enough that my fundamental research checks out on each stock. Stock price momentum needs to also be in an upward trend line over time. I want to invest in stocks that go up over the long run.

51. I verify net accumulation in a stock by checking its Accumulation / Distribution on StockCharts.com. If Accumulation / Distribution is rising along with its On-Balance Volume, especially in a stock that's consolidating (trading flat) and building a base, than that's a good sign. I want other people buying, and accumulating the stocks that I'm investing in too. It's all about the demand in its shares.

52. I do a new scan of North American stock markets – TSX, Venture, NYSE, and NASDAQ – at least every 3 months for new issues (IPOs). Also, some stocks appear on my filter for the very first time because they've finally surpassed a key metric benchmark, such as return on capital (ROIC). I'm always on top of the market, and screening for new growth opportunities. But I also manually browse through all company filings on SEDAR (Canadian filings database). I don't want companies to slip through my screens, and out of vision. Sometimes you have to conduct the manual work and sift through hundreds, upon thousands of company reports. It's not always about the numbers in a screen – you need to analyze the business.

53. I'll use leverage / margin in my portfolio, but won't let debt surpass 20% of my portfolio's total dollar value.

54. When I sell a declining stock on the basis that my original investment thesis was invalidated for whatever reason, I'll invest the proceeds into one of my winners. The winners can make up for any past losses and then some.

55. There's no such thing as passive investing if you're a DIY investor who's picking stocks. I'm checking my portfolio on a daily basis. If I wanted to 'buy and forget', I would cash out and put all of my money into an S&P 500 index fund / ETF. But that also means accepting those 'index-like' returns – I want to beat the market.

56. Losing money has been the best lesson for me. I know what to avoid now; companies, and management teams that destroy shareholder value. With experience I can more quickly identify and screen-out those bad companies. It's surprising how many companies are superb at capital *destruction*. But I also study other people's mistakes. It's cheaper. That includes mistakes made by hedge fund managers, and other "smart money". Nobody's right all the time. As James Altucher says, "the investors and hedge fund managers who are successful all of the time are probably criminals [insider trading] or about to lose everything". When investors – professional or DIY – get caught up in a "story stock" there's really no excuse. A suitable example is Timminco. Timminco was a hot "story stock" because it operated in the appealing alternative energy sector, selling silicon to solar energy manufacturers. The idea was that you could profit from the future surge in green technology by investing in Timminco, making you an instant millionaire *sarcasm*. As a result, Timminco's stock rose giddily from $0.33/share in 2006 to its all-time high of $34/share in 2008. Timminco's stock return was astronomical, but then dropped like a rock. At its 2008 peak, Timminco declined from $34/share to $0.50/share (2010), declaring bankruptcy in 2012. What went wrong? As its stock price shot up to the sun, Timminco's earnings were deteriorating (2006: $-0.33 EPS, 2007: $-0.20 EPS, 2008: $-0.09 EPS, 2009: $-0.83 EPS). Simply, investors became enchanted with Timminco's story, and not all stories have happy endings. A similar story stock – SunEdison – was part of a "Hedge Fund Hotel" years later, surging on a lot of the same euphoria around alternative energy.

57. Think about all the assets (intangible and tangible) that a company owns, and not only each assets' cash flow generation *now*, but its ability to generate cash flow in the *future*. Having a lot of assets on the balance sheet doesn't mean anything if the company can't continually generate a high return on those assets for its shareholders. I love companies with wonderful assets, especially intangible assets – like Disney. The worst management teams buy bad assets through acquisitions at too high a price, and then write off their mistakes (the bad assets) later. Management needs to be good stewards of capital for their shareholders.

58. I go to StockCharts.com on a daily basis, and check their free "Predefined Scans" section, to monitor any stocks hitting new 52-week highs. If I see companies hitting new 52-week highs, especially on a consecutive basis, I conduct further research and invest based on my aforementioned criteria. Why? Because that new 52-week high is break-through price momentum that is being fueled by high demand (investors and institutions buying shares), and so something might be going on. It's your job to find out.

Similarly, stocks that finally break out of a consolidation phase (flat-line) are interesting to consider, especially if you can get in before the breakout. For example, take a look at Alphabet's ("GOOGL") stock chart – it traded in a flat range (consolidation) from the beginning of 2014 through mid-2015, and then broke out on a stellar earnings report that beat analysts' expectations in July, 2015, surging from $550/share to close-to $1,000/share (2017), doubling its market capitalization in just two short years (~35% annual compound rate of return).

In his book, *How I Made 2,000,000 in the Stock Market*, Nicolas Darvas shares how he turned $10,000 into $2,450,000.00 in 18 months (1957-58 bull market) using his "BOX theory", which is based on monitoring price consolidations through a stock's rise. Darvas actively mapped a stock price's trend line into a series of boxes.

When the stock price was confined in a "box"; in other words, trading range-bound (consolidation), he waited, and then bought when the price rose out of the box (the upper most point in the price range). He would invest more every time the stock's price rose out of a new box, indicating new, and established "highs". Darvas simultaneously set a stop-loss just under this new stock price (which I don't recommend, because all growth stocks have minor corrections through their upwards trajectory).

Another interesting technical formation that I like to see (but is not mandatory) is the "Cup and Handle". Generally, I could look for a bit of a run-up, then consolidation, and then a sell-off in a stock, so that the run-up makes the edge of the cup, the consolidation makes the top of the cup, and then the sell-off makes the handle, marking the point before it might takeoff. From there, if the stock breaches the consolidation point then that can signal a decent move higher, but certainly isn't a guarantee. Interestingly, because some technical patterns and indicators are now so universally known, they might be self-fulfilling.

Some other technical patterns (you can study):

- Pennant
- Hammer
- Falling Wedge
- Inside Day
- Bull Flag
- Symmetrical Triangle
- Holy Grail Setup

59. I never say, "shoot – I missed out on that stock", if I see that it's gone up 500% in 5 years, for example.

Especially if it's still a micro-cap, small-cap or mid-cap company, because I know that those great, and still small companies can compound many times more. As I've said before, I also never say, "It's too expensive so I won't buy the stock", after simply looking at the price-to-earnings ratio (P/E) and nothing more. Why? The stock market is forward-looking.

60. I don't quickly overlook companies that aren't generating a profit. They may be the next winners on the stock market. By the time Amazon started to generate a consistent profit, it had already become a $400+ billion dollar company, compounding many times over, and making some shareholders incredibly wealthy, but leaving others on the sideline who said, "I still don't know how to evaluate the damn thing". Small companies are investing everything back into the business so don't always expect profit early on, but at least positive cash flows.

61. When I hear that there's been a change of management in a company, I will take a second look especially if I skipped over the company in the past. The new management might be better operators and capital allocators, taking the company to new heights.

62. I avoid companies that only grow through unsustainable, and manufactured inorganic growth, (i.e., acquisitions, fueled by debt), because once the debt, or acquisition opportunities dry up (and often it's both), the stock will fall straight to the ground for value investors to scoop up. Acquiring companies and doing just that isn't a business strategy; it's a scheme.

63. I like to learn about how successful investors think; their framework on why and how they pick stocks. You can read my book, *Market Masters*, as well as *The Money Train*, or *Market Wizards*, to get into the minds of top investors.

64. There's little spread to be made in merger-arbitrage these days because of high frequency trading, and easily accessible information. The rare case there is a juicy spread, the takeover could very well fall through. Take a look at the failed Ontario Teachers' Pension Plan / Bell Canada takeover case. Investors in that merger-arbitrage play got crushed on a deal that seemed like a "sure thing". To explain merger arbitrage; when Company A announces its purchase of Company B for x amount, Company B's stock price will rise close to but not exactly at the announced x amount. That's because there's still the risk the deal won't actually close, combined with the existence of "time value of money" or in other words, opportunity cost – investors could have their money tied up elsewhere. What one can then do is purchase stock in Company B, wait until the deal finally closes, and then collect the spread (when it actually goes up to price x). It sounds simple but, again, you need to assess the probability of the deal actually closing as it was announced to the public. So, I'd rather conduct my own research, and invest in micro-cap, and small cap companies that could soon possibly be taken over. These are my "speculative takeovers". For example, I purchased shares in Rona, speculating that Lowe's would return to attempt another takeover, having been blocked the first time by the Quebec Government. Lowe's did come back and succeeded in their second takeover attempt, sending Rona's stock up 100% in one day. Nice payday.

65. I've come to realize that the market is largely

psychologically-driven. John Maynard Keynes described the stock market as a Keynesian Beauty Contest, where "it is not a case of choosing those [faces] that, to the best of one's judgment, are really the prettiest, nor even those that average opinion genuinely thinks the prettiest. We have reached the third degree where we devote our intelligences to anticipating what average opinion expects the average opinion to be". This 'beauty contest' can be demonstrated in what I'll coin, in an homage to "The Nifty Fifty", "The Sexy Six": Facebook, Apple, Alphabet, Netflix, Tesla, and Amazon – 5 of which I own in my own portfolio.

66. I compare my long ideas (stocks I want to buy) with their current short positions (as a % of float) and the accompanying analyses by any prominent short sellers. I always want to take into account the reasons why others would want to short a stock (i.e., bet that it will fall in price). For instance, investors who were long Home Capital stock 2015 – 2017 would have done themselves a big favour by reading what prominent short seller, Marc Cohodes, had to say about the company. While it's certainly hard to sell when a stock has achieved such stellar share price performance, as in the case of Home Capital, one has to play devil's advocate to be successful over the long run. I don't just complacently say, "How could anything ever go wrong? Look at the stock chart. It's a great business." Here's a glimpse into how Marc Cohodes thinks before he shorts a company like Home Capital:

"I never, ever, ever get involved in what I would call open-ended situations. . . . I have avoided pie-in-the-sky names. To use an analogy, I'm not interested in climbing into a tree and wrestling the jaguar out of the tree. I'm

interested in someone shooting the jaguar out of the tree, and then I will go cut the thing apart once it hits the ground. Instead of open-ended situations, I like to short complete pieces of garbage with fraudulent management and horrifically bad balance sheets. I look for change, I look for 'if this goes away tomorrow will anyone miss them'? What do they do well?"

While I compare my long ideas against shorts, I never actually short stocks that I think will go down. I understand that while I can achieve more than a 100% return in a stock by going long (buying stock), I can only make 100% or less by shorting a stock.

67. Usually the media headlines (e.g. "The Death of Equities" or "Sell Canada") are most depressing exactly before the market starts to turn up again after a recession, bear market, or correction. This makes for a great buying opportunity, which is why I keep cash on-hand (and still read news headlines as a contrarian indicator). Here's an example: in Canada, on January 20, 2016, Maclean's published a feature article, "Assume the Crash Position: How far will the stock market fall? Canada's stock market has suffered through a lost decade of returns. Why the bad times for Canadian investors could continue".

This is what Maclean's Magazine had to say:

"...the glory days for Canada's stock market—when the S&P/TSX could be relied upon to outperform the U.S. S&P 500, as it did immediately following the financial crisis— are as good as dead. With global markets now faltering, too, Canadian investors are left wondering just how bad things will get... the outlook appears to be getting worse, not better." Well, just weeks later, in February, 2016,

Canada's stock markets – TSX and Venture Exchange – started to rocket upwards, surpassing other markets around the world that year. This reversal reminded me of what Bob Dylan said in his song, *The Times They Are A-Changin'*: "For the loser now, will be later to win", and of course, Warren Buffett's adage came to mind: be "fearful when others are greedy and greedy when others are fearful".

Similarly, in the August 13th, 1979 issue of Business Week, the cover story heralded "The Death of Equities".

The introduction stated:

"The masses long ago switched from stocks to investments having higher yields and more protection from inflation. Now the pension funds – the market's last hope-- have won permission to quit stocks and bonds for real estate, futures, gold, and even diamonds. The death of equities looks like an almost permanent condition-- reversible someday, but not soon." I'm sure you can guess what happened next… (yes – stocks went back up.)

68. If I'm buying particular stocks and see that other small-cap funds or hedge funds are buying the same stocks too, that gives me some validation. But it doesn't mean they'll work out. Just because they're professional money managers, doesn't mean they're always making smart decisions. Some DIY investors might choose to 'ride the coattails', meaning they could purposefully invest in what top investors buy in the stock market. Bill Ackman, billionaire hedge fund manager (Pershing Square), said in *Market Masters*: "You can't necessarily buy at the [top investors'] price, but once they announce the investment you can invest in it alongside them. And oftentimes stocks don't go straight up, so there's an opportunity to buy it again at a cheaper price." Some of the funds that I follow, which also invest in small-and-mid-cap Canadian stocks are: Turtle Creek Asset Management, Pender Funds, Giverny Capital, Donville Kent Asset Management, JC Clark Adaly Trust, and Mawer New Canada Fund. You can validate U.S. stock ideas with these top investors' funds through their 13F filings on Whale Wisdom: Dalal Street, Third Point, ValueAct, Arlington Value Capital, Akre Capital Management, Tweedy Browne, Trian, Omega, Wedgewood SQ, and Pershing Square. I also follow analysts like Gerry Wimmer (who I'll cover in a later chapter on small technology stocks). My portfolio has some overlap with these above funds but I don't indiscriminately copy their picks. I conduct my own research and stay independent.

69. There's always tail risk. Someday, when you're not expecting, some event will rock the stock market, sending it sharply downwards. But we'll only know about it *after-the-fact*, because unfortunately we don't own a functioning crystal ball. I don't worry about things that I can't control. Thus, I control risk by holding great stocks and managing what I can in my portfolio. Here's some ways that investors can control risk: keep cash on hand, buy puts (e.g. S&P 500 puts), control position size (i.e. invest more money as a % of your portfolio in more 'sure things', and less money in smaller, or new companies that have yet to prove themselves to you), and set stop-losses on individual stocks – but I don't recommend stop losses, and am only sharing them with you so that you know they exist.

70. I don't rush into an Initial Public Offering (IPO) the first day a company issues shares on the stock market. The problem is that IPOs are released to the retail investor only after institutions have claimed large blocks of shares for themselves at more attractive prices, so it's best to wait it out for some time. For example, Facebook; its stock dropped considerably after IPO day, from $38 to $19/share in 2012 (-50%), flat-lining through most of 2013, before breaking out and then going on a winning streak from $25 (2013) to $150/share (2017), achieving a 600% (7-bagger) return for shareholders. It's gone even higher since. The lesson here is to keep IPOs on your watchlist and monitor them for at least the first 3 months before you invest in them. There's no rush. Tesla flat-lined after its IPO in 2010 for 3 years, trading range-bound between $17 and $25/share, before it broke out in 2013, going from $25 (2013) to $310/share (2017), achieving 12-bagger status in four short years. Currently, Tesla is only trading around a $50 billion market capitalization, so I wouldn't be surprised to see the stock double again to $100 billion market cap as it grows its business, which now includes electric cars, power walls, batteries, and consumer solar panels. I find it very tough to bet against a visionary like Elon Musk.

71. Spin-offs (e.g. Yum Brands, which was spun off from PepsiCo, and owns KFC, Taco Bell, and Pizza Hut), are very interesting opportunities, because they are already proven businesses that can grow bigger on the public equity market as an independent company. Sometimes it takes activist investors like Bill Ackman to push a company's board of directors to spin-off subsidiaries to unlock value, as he did with Tim Hortons' spin-off from Wendy's International. In *Market Masters*, Ackman said: "If there's one business making $2 billion and another business, or another subsidiary, losing $1 billion, people will look at it and say, 'Oh, it's got $1 billion of earnings.' But that's not the right way to think about it." If you can identify that a company's parts are greater than its sum, you may have caught on to a future spinoff opportunity, such as was the case with Tim Horton's, which finally unlocked significant value for Tim Hortons, and its shareholders. As its own separate entity on the stock exchange, Tim Hortons flourished with expanded shareholder ownership and increased support from institutions and analysts. You can capitalize long into the post-breakup. For example, spinoffs will often outperform their parent companies in the long run, years after the spin-off. However, as with IPOs, there's usually a "cleansing period" for spin-offs, where existing shareholders of the parent company receiving spun-off stock in the new company may sell that new stock, sending the price down for some time. For example, Paypal, which was spun-off from eBay. For two years, Paypal stock was under selling pressure, as it traded range-bound around $40/share, before breaking out in 2017, and making new highs since.

72. The stock market exists to help companies raise capital, grow, and be successful. Why would I invest in bad companies that don't grow? That's what value investors do but that's not why the market exists. Remember, one of Warren Buffett, and Benjamin Graham's best investments, GEICO, was a growth stock! How ironic that two "value investors" invested in a growth company. The great blog, *Base Hit Investing*, documented that "Graham invested nearly 25% of his partner's capital into GEICO in 1948, acquiring 50% of the growing enterprise for the small sum of just $712,000. This would eventually grow to over $400 million 25 years later!! That is a 500-bagger". In fact, Benjamin Graham, the father of value investing, conceded later in his career that value investing wasn't what it used to be: "I am no longer an advocate of elaborate techniques of security analysis in order to find superior value opportunities. his was a rewarding activity, say, 40 years ago, when our textbook 'Graham and Dodd' was first published; but the situation has changed a great deal since then". It's true; with constant, and rapid change that effects business models, and in turn future cash flows, as well as a business' terminal value, value investing today (in the Graham-sense) is a lot like digging through the old discount DVD bins at Walmart. Even when you found the best DVDs in *that* bin, they were still bad movies. Those DVDs were in that bin for a reason. The great movies were always in the aisle, up on the shelf, marked at full price – and they all still attracted willing buyers.

In summary, these "72 Rules on Investing in Stocks" help me navigate the stock market and stay on track. If I'm not beating the market's long term return, (TSX ~10%), or beating it the majority of the time, then I should stop investing in individual equites and instead be putting my money into an index fund. It's been 13 years (2005 – 2018) and I'm still actively picking stocks, generating a 15% compound annual return in my portfolio. Hopefully I can keep it up. Because at a ~ 15% compound annual return, I can double my money around every 5 years (remember the rule of 72?), without taking on too much risk in the market.

✪ CHAPTER 4 ✪
(PART 1/2)
CAPITAL COMPOUNDERS – 25
MARKET BEATING STOCKS

As I mentioned in this book's introduction, I was invited to the Fairfax Financial Holdings (FFH) Shareholder's Dinner in 2017. It was there that I gave a popular talk on "Canadian Capital Compounders Today – 25 Market Beating Stocks". The FFH Shareholder's Dinner was on April 19th, and on April 20th was the Annual FFH Shareholder's Conference, otherwise known as the "Fairfax Lollapalooza". Prem Watsa's (Founder and CEO of Fairfax Financial) big day every year is commonly compared to Warren Buffett / Berkshire Hathaway's Annual Shareholder Conference, which has been coined "Woodstock for Capitalists", and attended by thousands.

Looking back on this talk; it really forced me to bring together all of the elements of my investment philosophy into a concise message. The "72 Rules" in the previous chapter may have been tough to read, and all over the place, but my talk on "Capital Compounders" is much more structured, and is the basis of my core investment philosophy. Throughout this chapter, you'll learn more about what growth stocks ("Capital Compounders") have in common and can use this information to find the next Capital Compounders in the future.

***

Canadian Capital Compounders Today– 25 Market Beating Stocks, Fairfax Financial Shareholder's Dinner, *April 19, 2017*

The Maple Leafs… If the Maple Leafs were publicly traded on the TSX they'd be in bubble territory. Too much euphoria. And too much downside. I wouldn't buy. But perhaps I'm dead wrong and the Maple Leafs have been a "value stock" all these years.

Hi everyone, my name is Robin Speziale, and I'm the National Bestselling author of *Market Masters: Interviews with Canada's Top Investors*.

Tonight I'll be talking about Canadian Capital Compounders Today – 25 Market Beating Stocks.

I'm a growth investor. Growth at a Reasonable Price, which means that I'll invest in a company trading at 30 P/E if its EPS growth rate is 30% or higher, for example. I say this because most so called "value investors" would just balk at that 30 P/E and move on. But I especially love finding Capital Compounders; those stocks in the small-cap and mid-cap space that eventually grow into large-caps, on the foundation of their exceptional wealth creating ability, fueled by expanding book value per share, earnings per share, and free cash flow per share.

The challenge, though, is finding these Capital

Compounders when they're small. For example, I'm certain some of you probably found Fairfax Financial Holdings (FFH) when it was a much smaller, and largely unknown company around the year 2000. But most investors at that time were likely thinking about stocks such as Bombardier, Loblaw, and CIBC; those large caps with less runway for growth but more analyst coverage, institutional ownership, and retail investor awareness. However, as Peter Lynch said: "The person that turns over the most rocks wins the game." By the way, if you did invest in Fairfax Financial Holdings (FFH) shares in 2000, well done, because you're up 235%, beating the TSX's 64% return over that same period, as well as the performance of those three aforementioned large-cap stocks.

The list behind me [see the table below], is of 25 exceptional Canadian Capital Compounders; many of which I hold in my own stock portfolio. They're all still publicly traded on the TSX. I don't include past top Capital Compounders like Paladin Labs, which under Jonathan Goodman's leadership, was close-to a 100-bagger (100x return)... in other words delivering a 9,900% cumulative return. $1.50 invested in Paladin Labs at its founding was worth $142 nineteen years later. Amazing. And so are these 25 market beating Capital Compounder stocks:

Company	CEO / Founder	Compound Annual Return
CRH Medical	Edward Wright	82.38%
Dollarama	Larry Rossy	55.53%
New Flyer Industries	Paul Soubry Jr.	43.33%
Computer Modelling	Ken Dedeluk	41.80%
Constellation Software	Mark Leonard	38.18%
Premium Brands	George Paleologou	29.68%
Stella-Jones	Brian McManus	26.92%
Alimentation Couche-Tard	Alain Bouchard	26.78%
Tucows	Elliot Noss	26.57%
Savaria	Marcel Bourassa	25.13%
MTY Food Group	Stanley Ma	22.25%
Gildan Activewear	Glenn J. Chamandy	20.72%
Stantec	Robert Gomes	20.34%
Pollard Banknote	Douglas Pollard	19.94%
Richelieu Hardware	Richard Lord	19.82%
CCL Industries	Geoffrey Martin	18.09%
Metro	Eric R. La Flèche	17.87%
Saputo	Lino A. Saputo Jr.	17.66%
Lassonde Industries	Jean Gattuso	16.77%
Canadian National Railway	Luc Jobin	15.77%
TFI International	Alain Bedard	15.38%
Photon Control	Scott Edmonds	14.76%
Brookfield Asset Management	Bruce Flatt	13.21%
Enghouse Systems	Stephen J. Sadler	12.05%
Logistec	Madeleine Paquin	10.30%

*Compound Annual Return in the table above is calculated since inception on the TSX (for each company), through April 10, 2017.

You can download the full spreadsheet of these 25 Canadian Capital Compounder Stocks on RobinSpeziale.com (filename: *Canadian Capital Compounders – Robin Speziale – Market Masters – 2017*), which includes the Company, CEO / Founder, Return on Capital (last 5 years), Compound Annual Return, Cumulative Return, and Number of Years on the Market.

To the average stock picker, not all of these 25 companies will be known, but their returns, nonetheless, have been market-beating; all compounding at rates higher than the S&P/TSX's long term 9.8% compound annual return. The average compound annual return among these 25 stocks is 26%, based on each stock's return since inception on the TSX. An average 26% compound annual return is outstanding in and of itself, but even more so because it does not include dividends; just capital appreciation alone. I have realized that there's a strong correlation in the long run in a company's return on capital (ROIC) and its share price performance (compound annual returns). The average ROIC of these 25 capital compounder stocks is 16% (that's over the last 5 years).

To name a handful of these exceptional Canadian Capital Compounder stocks today: Dollarama, Constellation Software, Alimentation Couche-Tard, Savaria, MTY Food Group, CCL Industries, and Lassonde Industries. It's important to note that you won't see any oil & gas, resource, or mining companies on this list. I call companies in those sectors "capital destroyers" over the long run. They're cyclical price-takers, meaning their prospects are dependent largely on prevailing commodity prices (e.g. barrel of oil, or ounce of gold, etc.). Sometimes the key to successful investing is simply knowing what to avoid, cutting out the bottom 80-20% of the market. Capital intensive businesses – oil & gas, resource, mining – aslo operate in highly competitive industries and thus possess no competitive advantage. Another case in point; the airline industry. Cash continually needs to be reinvested into maintenance costs and new airplanes, stalling any growth, and so airline companies will never really take flight in your portfolio for a sustained period.

Some of these 25 Capital Compounder companies still likely have considerable runway to grow, whereas others won't have as much growth ahead because of the law of large numbers. Obviously, a company cannot compound at the same high rate forever. For example, Brookfield Asset Management, which is a large $48 billion dollar company. But that's not to say that Brookfield has no more runway, as it continues to gobble up public infrastructure.

So, what are the commonalities of these 25 Capital Compounder stocks? It would be great to use this knowledge so that you can find the next ones…

I'll first reference Chuck Akre's "three legged stool" – the three foundations of "compounding machines", as he calls them. Akre, an influence on me, founded Akre Capital Management, coining the term compounding machines to describe businesses that are capable of compounding shareholders' capital at high rates for long periods with little risk of permanent loss of capital. Plus he came up with a brilliant visualization to illustrate his philosophy; "the three-legged stool". Aker actually has a stool in his office's main boardroom as a constant reminder:

"The first leg of the stool has to do with the business models that are likely to compound the shareholders' capital at above-average rates, combined with leg two, people who run the business who are not only exceptional at running the business but also see to it that what happens at the company level also happens at the per share level– and then leg three, where because of the nature of the business and the skill of the manager there is both history as well as an opportunity to reinvest all the excess capital they generate in places where they earn these above-average rates of return."

On Chuck's last point, "reinvesting all the excess

capital", we know that CEOs really have 5 choices in deploying capital: 1) invest back in their business, 2) acquire / integrate new businesses, 3) buy back shares, 4) pay down debt, 5) issue and / or raise a dividend. Outstanding companies do the first three incredibly well; re-invest back into their business, acquire / integrate great companies, and buy back shares at opportune prices over time. In my opinion, and this isn't true in all cases, but companies that payout a large amount of dividends (high dividends yields), concede that they can't deploy that cash as effectively back into their business to earn high rates of return anymore. This is true of most large-caps, with some exceptions to that rule included in this list. Why? Because management still invests back into the business, as there remains re-investment opportunities for ample return.

So, to conclude, the following are the key commonalities of these 25 Canadian Capital Compounders, which have all beaten the market (TSX):

- Free cash-flow generative, high return on capital businesses (16% ROIC – last 5 year average);
- Run by exceptional operators, and shareholder-oriented managers (with stake in the business) who;
- Effectively deploy capital to grow their business, continually delivering high rates of return for their shareholders (26% Compound Annual Return average)

Some of these exceptional managers, who are not only effective capital allocators, but also incredible operators, are Larry Rossy (Dollarama), Mark Leonard (Constellation Software), Stanley Ma (MTY Food Group), Alain

Bouchard (Alimentation Couche-Tard), and Bruce Flatt (Brookfield Asset Management).

But perhaps most importantly, these 25 Capital Compounder companies have demonstrated sustainable competitive advantages, whether that be through the industries in which they operate, their operating models, distribution network, niche products / services, regulatory advantages, patents, technology, or brand / goodwill. Not only does durable competitive advantage allow these companies to compound shareholder wealth over a long period of time, but they have strong and enduring balance sheets capable of funding growth, and avoiding crashing in economic downturns. Indeed, these 25 Capital Compounders seem to have staying power, as their average public life is 15 years on the market (TSX), with hopefully more years of out-performance to follow.

To recap, these 25 Capital Compounders data:

- Average compound return (since inception): 26%
- Average ROIC (over last 5 years): 16%
- Average public life (so far): 15 years

[Note: Compound Annual Return was based on capital appreciation returns since inception for each stock on the Toronto Stock Exchange (S&P/TSX), up to April 10, 2017. The Return on Capital (ROIC) 5-year average is from 2011 – 2016, sourced from Morningstar.com.]

Post-talk Thought: While my favourite holding period is forever, I understand that businesses have lifecycles too. And so it's important that as DIY investors, we always stay active in the market, diligently monitoring the stocks in our portfolios. These 25 Capital Compounders won't grow at the same high rate forever, and some might be disrupted in the next 10 years (maybe sooner). The point of the talk was to celebrate these companies, but more importantly to highlight their key qualities – so that you can leverage this knowledge to find the next Capital Compounders.

Nothing is forever. Disruption happens. So let's review an example from the list of 25 Capital Compounder stocks – Alimentation Couche-Tard – examining its future growth plan, and how it might maintain its competitive advantage. You should review each company in your portfolio like this every year, trying to find any cracks in its armour.

I would say that based on public management commentary, Alimentation Couche-Tard, a gas station and convenience store operator, is currently hunting for assets in Asia to expand into new markets. However, what I'm mostly concerned and anxious about is understanding management's vision to adapt to, and grow along with disruption in the industry, especially with the proliferation of electric, and self-driving vehicles. Future transportation can impact consumer behavior among traffic to Alimentation's gas stations spread across North America, and Europe. Imagine; if you don't have to fuel up your car with gasoline at a standard gas station (because you drive electric), then you won't have the opportunity to go into their stores to buy anything. Also, our increasingly 'on-demand' economy means more consumers will buy online and have things delivered to them. We're seeing this change in consumer behavior with fast food (e.g. Uber Eats), and we might see this behavior with small purchases too, like chocolate bars, and drinks sooner than we think. Who really knows. Finally, with cigarette sales in decline for decades (can marijuana products take their place?), convenience stores have relied on lottery ticket sales, directly and indirectly (brings people into the stores to buy other things). That steady, reliable traffic might change in the future too. Alimentation Couche-Tard (ATD.B) stock has been consolidating over the past couple of years after a great run up in price. And while an acquisition and continued earnings growth will push the stock up, I believe investors have the same thought: how will Alimentation grow amongst this rapid pace of change? Management's answer to this question, and subsequent execution will determine the next meaningful period of growth in the stock.

***

Well, I hope you enjoyed my original talk on Capital Compounders; learning about those 25 market beating stocks, and my assessment of the three main commonalities that fueled their share price out-performance.

Interestingly, later that year I met a gentleman through a friend who from 1982 to 2000 ran a $1B technology fund in the U.S.. These days he was investing in U.S. Capital Compounders. "John", I'll call him, was in Toronto visiting family for the Christmas holidays, and lived in San Francisco with his wife. Amazingly, before running the fund, he was a part of Apple's IPO underwriting team, and then while running the fund, John met Bill Gates and was one of Microsoft's first institutional investors. John retired in 2001, and has been running his own personal stock portfolio since, with a focus on U.S. Capital Compounders.

Our meeting was at Starbucks (a remarkable stock!), and he scribbled down his current holdings – see photo below. While he was previously only an investor in the technology sector, as that was his fund's mandate, he now buys stocks in pretty much any industry (except the cyclical ones), with an intense focus on high growth, and high return on capital.

While 80% of my portfolio is in Canadian stocks, I had some overlap with John's U.S. picks in the remaining 20%. Indeed, Capital Compounder stocks can be found all around the world – U.S., Canada, U.K., China, etc., using the same screening methodology that I described in my talk on "Capital Compounders". Interestingly, John still doesn't own any Canadian stocks in his portfolio, so I encouraged him to research three Canadian Capital Compounders as a start: Tucows, Constellation Software, and Savaria.

John's U.S. Capital Compounders (December, 2017)

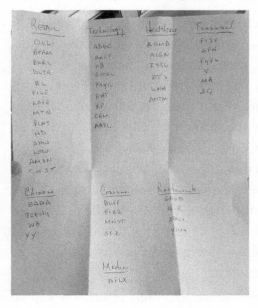

✪ CHAPTER 5 ✪
(PART 2/2)
NEXT CAPITAL COMPOUNDERS
– 15 ADDITIONAL GROWTH
STOCKS

In Part ½ of the chapter on "Capital Compounders", I wrote about how I was invited to speak at the Annual Fairfax Financial Shareholder's Dinner on April 19, 2017. It was a pretty big deal for me, as the company's Founder & CEO Prem Watsa, who some call the "Buffett of Canada", was in the audience. My speech was on "Canadian Capital Compounders Today – 25 Market Beating Stocks", discussing the key attributes that all these stocks had in common to explain their outperformance:

- Mostly small-mid caps ($100M – $10B) in the non-cyclical Technology, Consumer, and Diversified Industries space – large addressable markets and long growth runways;

- Free cash-flow generative, high return on capital businesses (with a durable moat);

- Run by exceptional operators (with a stake in the business), and shareholder-oriented managers who;

- Effectively deploy capital into investment opportunities (invest back into the business, acquire / integrate smaller companies, and buy back shares over time), continually delivering high rates of return for their shareholders

I said: "I like to think that there's a strong correlation in the long run between a company's Return on Capital (ROIC) and its share price performance... the average ROIC of these 25 Capital Compounder stocks is 16% (5 year average)... and the average compound annual return [since each company's trading inception on the TSX] is 26%". Looking back, this might have not been the best comparison; comparing the 25 Capital Compounders' past 5 years average ROIC with past *15+* years (average) share price performance, but it was important to make the abstract connection. Later in this chapter, I'll show the shorter 2017-2018 period share price performance (1 Year) since my original Capital Compounders talk vs. ROIC (5 Year Average), and discuss whether there was in fact a correlation. The conclusion I want to validate: do high return on capital companies "Capital Compounders" actually generate more wealth (share price appreciation) for investors, and can a basket of these superior companies beat the market (S&P/TSX)?

It had been over one year since my talk on these 25 Capital Compounders, and so I wanted to gauge their stock performance over that period, reflecting on both my process, and justification for picking this particular group of stocks. The results were satisfactory. In aggregate, the 25 Canadian Capital Compounders (see Table 1 below) achieved a +15.8% return from April 19, 2017 to June 29,

2018, easily beating the S&P/TSX (+4.7%), and ranking closely alongside the S&P 500 (+17.2%), and DJIA (+19.9%). Further, it was encouraging to see that for Year-to-Date (YTD) 2018 (January – June), this basket of 25 Capital Compounders was up +5.7%, ahead of all three comparison indexes; S&P/TSX (+0.4%), S&P 500 (+1.7%), and DJIA (-1.8%). The performance comparison summary can be found further below in Table 2.

Table 1: Original 25 Capital Compounders

Company	Ticker	'17 – '18 Return	YTD '18 Return
Pollard Banknote	PBL	104.80%	25.30%
Constellation Software	CSU	62.20%	34.70%
Photon Control	PHO	56.70%	27.00%
Logistec	LGT	50.30%	20.80%
TFI International	TFII	37.30%	23.10%
Enghouse Systems	ENGH	34.40%	24.90%
Premium Brands	PBH	32.30%	10.10%
Dollarama	DOL	30.90%	-0.80%
Lassonde Industries	LAS	15.40%	12.30%
Stella-Jones	SJ	11.10%	-4.60%
Brookfield Asset Management	BAM	9.20%	-0.60%
Canadian National Railway	CNR	9.10%	3.40%
Savaria	SIS	8.10%	-14.00%
CCL Industries	CCL	7.90%	12.40%
Metro	MRU	7.40%	10.90%
Tucows	TC	4.40%	2.40%
MTY Food Group	MTY	2.50%	-10.50%
Gildan Activewear	GIL	0.50%	-7.90%
Saputo	SAP	-2.20%	-2.90%
New Flyer Industries (NFI)	NFI	-2.50%	-9.50%
Stantec	STN	-2.60%	-4.00%
Alimentation Couche-Tard	ATD	-5.10%	-11.90%
Richelieu Hardware	RCH	-5.20%	-20.60%
Computer Modelling Group	CMG	-5.60%	4.10%
CRH Medical	CRH	-66.20%	17.70%

Table 2: Performance Summary ("Capital Compounders" vs. Comparison Indexes)

Index	Apr '17 – Jun '18	YTD 2018
S&P/TSX	4.70%	0.40%
S&P 500	17.20%	1.70%
DJIA	19.90%	-1.80%
Capital Compounders	15.80%	5.70%

The top three performers over that 2017 – 2018 period were Pollard Banknote (+104.8%), Constellation Software (+62.2%), and Photon Control (+56.7%), and the top 10 (out of 25) stocks delivered an average 43.5% return.

Interestingly, the top three performers YTD 2018 were the same 3 stocks from the 2017 – 2018 period, demonstrating that performance trends can prevail. "The trend is your friend", as they say. If I remove the worst performer from the group (CRH Medical), the 2017-2018 average return is 19.2%, but if I remove the best performer (Pollard Banknote), it's 12.1%. I also observed that around 80% of these stocks seemed to be in a multi-year consolidation phase. Thus, I wouldn't hesitate to personally invest more at these share price levels, as there's a near-term opportunity for some stocks to break out of their bases – hopefully higher, of course, but that's not certain.

One year after my original talk at the Fairfax Financial Dinner (April, 2017) on 25 Capital Compounders, I found that there was indeed a correlation between these 25 stocks' Return on Capital (16% ROIC; 5 Year Average) and their share price performance (+15.8%). While this correlation won't always be achieved in the short term, and can be due to a mix of other factors, High ROIC = High Share Price Performance, should theoretically play out in the long run.

But nothing is certain. Companies come and go, and markets can surprise us.

This is why it's so important to always be on the quest for new Capital Compounders. As a DIY investor, one needs to continually keep their portfolio fresh with small-to-mid cap growth stocks, and also micro-cap stocks, which I'll talk about in a later chapter – *Small Companies; Big Dreams*. I'm not saying to sell long-held stocks at 'the top', because as we know, high can go higher, which is the desired outcome in our wealth-building journey. But rather, I'm suggesting that one supplements his portfolio (which might now include large-caps) with new ideas. Obviously, based on the law of large numbers a company cannot compound at the same high rate forever. I used Brookfield Asset Management as an example in the original talk, which can't as easily or quickly double many more times over at this point in its life. Plant new seeds, and water the growing trees (winners).

To this end, I've posted below the "Next 15 Canadian Capital Compounders" for your consideration, which I'll supplement and track along with my original 25 Capital Compounders. So, now there's 40 "Canadian Capital Compounders". The majority of these 15 companies (see Table 3 below) are between Small-Cap ($100M – $2B) and Mid-Cap ($2B – $10B) in size, sharing the same attributes as discussed throughout (high ROIC, exceptional capital allocation, ample investment opportunities / returns, etc.). On a trailing twelve-month (TTM) basis from June, 2018, these 15 companies in aggregate achieved a 17.2% Return on Capital (ROIC), and over the last 5 years; 15.9% Average ROIC. Their average compound annual return (since inception on the TSX) is 23.3%, with an average public life of 14 years. Impressively, 5 (out of 15) companies below have achieved a 30%+ compound annual return on the stock market since their inception, with Kinaxis (+61%), Spin Master (+47%), and FirstService (+43%) ranking the highest in their ability to generate shareholder wealth since each company's inception (i.e., when they started trading on the TSX).

The 'newest' 6 companies (out of 15), with only 3-5 years of public trading on the TSX, are Spin Master (TOY), Fairfax India (FIH.U), Sleep Country (ZZZ), First Service (FSV), Kinaxis (KXS), and BRP (DOO). Some companies, like Transcontinental (TCL.B), have a much longer tenure on the stock market, but are transforming their business models for future growth, and so one might expect higher compound returns from this point on. In Transcontinental's case, management is transforming the business model from traditional newspapers / printing to shipping / packaging for the e-commerce age. Others in the list are larger companies (e.g. Magna) that are diversifying into new investment opportunities (AI, electric vehicles, etc.) to drive their next growth phase. However, the majority of companies below should fit into the small-mid-cap space, with large addressable markets, and long runways to grow.

Table 3: Next 15 Capital Compounders

Company	Ticker	CEO	ROIC (TTM)	ROIC (5yr Avg)
Spin Master	TOY	Ronnen Harary	31.60%	46.50%
BRP	DOO	Jose Boisjoli	30.90%	29.10%
Sylogist	SYZ	Jim Wilson	23.00%	13.50%
Tecsys	TCS	Peter Brereton	19.00%	11.60%
Calian Group	CGY	Kevin Ford	17.40%	17.00%

Transcontinental	TCL.B	François Olivier	16.30%	10.90%
Sleep Country	ZZZ	David Friesema	16.00%	12.20%
Magna International	MG	Donald J. Walker	15.90%	17.60%
Kinaxis	KXS	John Sicard	15.50%	18.40%
Fairfax India	FIH.U	Chandran Ratnaswami	14.50%	13.80%
CGI Group	GIB.A	George Schindler	12.60%	12.10%
Great Canadian Gaming	GC	Rod N. Baker	12.30%	12.00%
FirstService	FSV	D. Scott Patterson	11.30%	5.40%
CAE	CAE	Marc Parent	10.90%	9.20%
Andrew Peller	ADW.B	John E. Peller	10.40%	8.80%

*TTM = Trailing Twelve Months

I'll track these 40 Capital Compounders (25 + 15) for the foreseeable future, and I'll always be on the lookout for more as new companies IPO on the market, spin-off's happen, and old companies evolve. As I've said before, if I can achieve a 15% compound annual return in my portfolio over the long run, then I'm a happy guy. Striving for anything over 15% and I'm taking on too much risk and that can blow up my portfolio. Achieving anything below 15%, and I would rather just hold an Index ETF (e.g. S&P 500). A 15% compound annual return is the sweet spot, and means that I can double my money every 5 years, based on the Rule of 72.

Before I conclude, it's important to highlight again that I am not overly concerned with Price-to-Earnings multiples (P/E) over the long run as I'm a Growth-at-a-Reasonable-Price (GARP) investor. If I avoided companies with 30+ P/E over the past 13 years, I wouldn't have created much wealth at all in my portfolio. I'd just be sitting on my thumbs along with the other Bears (stock market pessimists), "waiting for a pullback" and investing in the likes of Torstar, Corus Entertainment, and Reitman's among other classic "value stocks" that teach one a very valuable lesson: cheap stocks can get cheaper. I also want to highlight that I use Return on Capital (ROIC) rather than Return on Equity (ROE) to ultimately base my investment decisions, as the latter metric can be inflated (i.e. look great!!) due to extensive debt leverage. I don't like debt, and I especially don't like companies that grow-by-excessive-leverage. See what happened to Valeant – look it up for an essential case study, knowing what to avoid in the future. I much prefer companies that are self-funded through their own free cash flow, combined with strong, well-capitalized balance sheets, so that those companies are capable of funding growth, and avoid crashing in economic downturns. This very important ROIC metric must be consistently high (which is why I use a minimum 5-year average), above a company's cost of capital, and preferably rising throughout the years, combined with growing revenues, book value per share, earnings per share, and free cash flow per share. The Return on Invested Capital (ROIC) definition, and calculation that I rely on can be found on Morningstar's website:

"The [ROIC] calculation is net operating profit after tax divided by average invested capital. The resulting figure is then multiplied by 100. Invested capital equals the sum of total stockholders' equity, long-term debt and capital lease obligation, and short-term debt and capital lease obligation. ROIC shows how much profit a company generates on its capital base. The better the company, the more profit it generates as a percentage of its invested capital..."

❂ CHAPTER 6 ❂
THINK SHORT: BECOMING A SMARTER LONG TERM INVESTOR

As I've said before, I've been investing in stocks for 13 years. I opened a brokerage account in my dorm room at the University of Waterloo in 2005, and have since built a $500,000 stock portfolio. But it's certainly not been easy. One of the most important things I've learned and accepted over time is that I will never achieve a perfect track record, or even close to perfect. Bagging winners 100% of the time is impossible. My portfolio will have losers now and losers in the future; a 60% success / win rate is my goal.

That being said, I've become a much better investor by limiting my blow-ups, whether that's through not selecting as many future under-performers, setting the right diversification (spreading my bets) or promptly selling out of a declining position in my portfolio that's violated my initial thesis (reason) for buying a stock. So, now I consider myself a perpetually skeptical buyer, meaning that I'm consciously, and decidedly not easily convinced. I have doubts and reservations about the markets, and stocks… all the time. I'm mindful about why I'm interested in a stock, and my interest won't ever be based on a tip, emotion, or a hunch, and especially not triggered from a broker, or analyst. The former can just as easily sell cars at a Ford dealership across the street (and should not be trusted), and the latter is simply a salary-man, whose job it is to begrudgingly cover companies in which he would otherwise have no interest in – it's his job.

I conduct my own extensive, and independent research on every stock before I initiate a new position in my portfolio so that the only person I can blame if something goes wrong is *me*. So, I'm skeptical. I honestly think that only 10% of the Canadian stock market is actually investable, with ~50 truly exceptional businesses. That same ratio (1 in 10 stocks are investable) can apply to the U.S. market too, but an even lower one applies to many international markets, where maybe 5% (1 in 20) of those stocks are actually "investable". Indeed, there's a lot of bad companies, and even more mediocre ones publicly traded on the stock market. I'm that skeptical.

Becoming an increasingly skeptical buyer has manifested through experience, and many money-losing lessons, which is why I'm now enthralled with the world of short sellers. People like Marc Cohodes, Carson Block, and Andrew Left who initiate shorts in companies; betting that a stock will fall in price, and then personally gaining if that scenario plays out in the market. Studying these prominent short sellers has improved my investing success. I integrate these short sellers' mindsets; always having on a skeptical lens through the stock screening process, and continually removing stocks from my universe that I'm skeptical about based on many of their short criteria. What remains in my watchlist, and in my portfolio, are companies in which I am *least* skeptical, and most knowledgeable about given all of the public information available to me at that time. That's really the best I can do because I've accepted that 'I don't know what I don't know'. I'll never know *everything* at all times about companies but I can adjust my positions based on new inputs that I learn over time.

If you meet someone who says they know *everything* about a company, they either have insider information, or are lying to your face. This is why I concentrate my portfolio in small-cap and mid-cap stocks where I feel I can have a *relative* informational edge because of both the low analyst coverage and institutional ownership in the space – there's simply not as many eyeballs on smaller companies.

Now that I'm a more skeptical buyer, before I initiate a new position, I always ask myself, "What can go wrong?". Because who wants to lose money? If I do initiate that position, I make an agreement with myself that I'll sell out of the position if there's any violation in my initial thesis, but not necessarily if the stock merely drops, as stock movements and company developments can sometimes be divorced, or at least not perfectly correlated with each other. Also, all growth stocks go through growing pains, and don't just shoot up. But I accept that things change. I can be wrong, and so I don't want to become emotional and be the guy who holds Nortel from $100+ down to $0.10.

Out of all of the well-known short sellers out there, I like Marc Cohodes the most. While he previously ran a hedge fund, he is not the typical 'silver spoon, pedigreed, private schooled guy' in the industry. He's rough around the edges, out-spoken, and now lives on a chicken farm, making short bets in his personal account that sometimes rock the market. Case in point – his short bet in Home Capital.

It's important to discuss Cohodes' framework here, so that you can use some of these short ideas in your own philosophy and stock selection process to become both a more skeptical buyer and owner of stocks in your portfolio.

I called up Marc Cohodes in the summer of 2017, when all eyes were on his Home Capital short bet. Marc was betting that the Canadian Housing market would soon collapse, taking Home Capital (secondary mortgage lender) down with it as mortgage originations dried up. Here's what Marc thinks about, and how he picks stocks to short (his own words):

"I never, ever, ever get involved in what I would call open-ended situations... I have avoided pie-in-the-sky names. To use an analogy, I'm not interested in climbing into a tree and wrestling the jaguar out of the tree. I'm interested in someone shooting the jaguar out of the tree, and then I will go cut the thing apart once it hits the ground. Instead of open-ended situations, I like to short complete pieces of garbage with fraudulent management and horrifically bad balance sheets. I look for change, I look for 'if this goes away tomorrow will anyone miss them'?... "

Marc usually bets on the jockey, not just the horse, meaning that unfortunately there's some pretty rotten managers out there. He focuses on companies that are "frauds, fads, or (impending) failures", stalks them (Marc calls himself a "stalker") until they're weak, and then finally pounces, initiating a short position; riding the stock down as it loses value, covering when the time is right, and making money through the process. Again, this thinking can help you in avoiding mistakes in the market and removing bad stocks from your portfolio. It's certainly helped me. Always be asking yourself:

- Is management good? Are they honest? Professional? (It's usually a waste time talking to management because they will usually give you a rosy picture of the company)
- Can this company potentially be a fraud (Enron), fad (Heelys), or failure (Blockbuster)?
- Does their product / service have staying power? (durable competitive advantage)
- Will I know the signs to look for when a company starts to turn for the worse? (especially on the balance sheet, and income statement – pay close attention to debt, revenue, and gross margin)
- Is there frequent accounting changes or obscurity in reporting? Are there overvalued assets on the balance sheet?
- Is the company constantly looking for new money; debt offerings, secondary stock offerings, etc.?
- If this company goes out of business tomorrow, will people miss their products or services? Or will nobody even care?
- Finally, if I do find something glaringly wrong in one of my stock holdings, do I have the emotional strength to pull the sell trigger?

Always be skeptical. But be flexible too. Treat small companies at the beginning of their business life cycle differently than large companies that are probably near, or at the end of their life cycle (unless they are constantly innovating, and disrupting themselves). I am more lenient with smaller companies – where big movements take time to develop (sometimes years after you invest) – that might be going through growing pains along their growth journey. On the other hand, I am more strict and less patient with larger companies. One must keep a watchful eye on large companies.

For example, take a look at this chart of Corus Entertainment (below). The stock is probably going to zero, unless an unfortunate buyer swoops in to completely buy it out. Otherwise, Corus will likely be liquidated (assets sold to multiple buyers), but not before more dividend cuts, and mass layoffs. Think about it; the few people who still even watch cable TV will pick American shows over Canadian shows. Corus Entertainment is a traditional TV, and radio content producer. The rapid pace of innovation, and shifting consumer taste in *what* people watch and *how* they access content are making Corus' offerings, and business model largely irrelevant today.

The lesson here is that times are always a-changing, and that a company needs to adapt or else it will die. Corus Entertainment was a good stock performer before the advent of Digital-TV, but now is struggling for survival. Skeptical investors would have sold, or never bought Corus in the first place understanding long ago this seismic shift taking place in the media industry. But "value" investors like to buy "cheap". Some poor saps probably thought

Corus Entertainment was a bargain back in 2014, trading at $25/share. As I'm writing this, Corus has dropped to $3.73/share. Ouch.

Yes – cheap can get cheaper, and cheaper, and cheaper. So, morale of the story is that one needs to remain skeptical at all times, and think rationally as a business owner when analyzing, and investing companies. Always look into the future, and don't become blinded by a low P/E, P/B, or high dividend yield, because those indicators are all based in the past. Stocks are usually cheap for a reason. Ask yourself: "Would anyone care if this business went away?... Would you care if Corus Entertainment went away?" Probably not! It's best to buy quality, and with quality stocks; you get what you pay for.

This is why I'm not a "value investor". There's a famous photo of famed Hedge Fund manager, Paul Tudor Jones relaxing in his office with his feet kicked up on his desk, with a single sheet of paper tacked on the wall behind him with just this phrase written out in black marker: *"Losers Average Losers"*. This phrase decries the act of what's taught in University and College Finance courses; "dollar-cost-averaging", where one would indiscriminately buy more of a stock as it drops in price. In reality, one would quickly find himself with a portfolio of losers by dollar-cost averaging so indiscriminately in the stock market.

As an side on Paul Tudor Jones, I encourage you to watch the rare documentary on him titled "Trader" (that's *if* you can find it, because "Trader" is very rare even on the internet). "Trader" was filmed about one year before the major market crash in 1987. In the documentary, Paul Tudor Jones said, in his southern U.S. drawl that "there will be some type of a decline, without a question, in the next 10, 20 months. And it will be earth-shaking; it will be saber-rattling." Sure enough, on October 19th, 1987, the U.S. market crashed – it was epic. The S&P 500 posted a 508-point (20%-plus) decline within hours. Paul Tudor Jones placed a short on the market and netted $100 million in profits on October 19, 1987. What an incredible bet!

Obviously, as a long-term investor you want to buy the stocks that go up, not the ones that keep going down. Some investors surprisingly are more skeptical when a stock is going up, because they call it "too expensive". Rubbish. Again, you get what you pay for, and it's egotistical to think that you are smarter than the market if and when you invest in a beaten-up company. By saying, "the market doesn't know how to appropriately price this stock", one is admitting their own arrogance. Jesse Livermore, legendary trader, echoed this sentiment: "markets are never wrong [but] opinions often are".

Rather than dollar cost averaging, I much prefer the practice of "averaging-up". But is there a systematic way of buying on the way up? I don't like a lot of technical analysis. But I do look at these indicators (source – StockCharts.com Predefined Scans): Accumulation Distribution, On-Balance Volume, 50/200 Day Moving Averages, Trend Lines, RSI, and MACD. What I really like, though, is the Darvas Box Theory.

The Darvas Box Theory is a way in which you can visualize your stocks' cycle; leg-up, then consolidation, then breakout (of box), then leg-up, and repeat again. Darvas was a dancer (odd for an investor, I know), but accumulated a fortune in the stock market; around $2,000,000 in his personal account from what I've read. On initiating new positons in stocks, Darvas outlined this plan:

- The fundamental analysis of the stock is promising
- The stock makes a new high
- Enter the stock as price trades through its all-time price level
- As the stock is trading up through its previous high, volume is surging

If you're interested in reading more on technical trading and investing, which I use to inform some of my new purchases, and also get updates on the trading activity among my current holdings, you can read these books:

1. Technical Analysis of the Futures Markets
2. Technical Analysis Explained
3. Elliott Wave Principle
4. "Comparative Study" in The Encyclopedia of Technical Market Indicators

Moral of the story: remain skeptical throughout your DIY investing journey. Be more skeptical with large companies than you are with smaller companies, because while one company might be going through growing pains, the other might be entering its end-of life stage. Buy stocks that go up, and buy more on the way up. Admittedly, this is easier said than done, as companies go through cycles, but is a good principle to keep in mind. I RARELY if ever dollar cost average. I got burned so bad on doing that in RIM / Blackberry when I was young that I learned a very good lesson; I could've been buying Apple on the way up. Guess what? I was more skeptical in Apple on the way up, than I was in BlackBerry / RIM on the way down. This was a behavioural error, which I'll discuss within a later chapter in this book on *Psychology*. So, be more skeptical about stocks that go down, than you are in stocks that go up.

While one must remain skeptical about individual companies in his portfolio, it never pays to be skeptical near the end of a systemic market crash that drags down with it even great companies. That's when I become overly enthusiastic to increase my stake in great companies at cheaper prices. It's like a huge bargain sale at your local grocery store, where everything is 30-50% off!

Becoming a more skeptical buyer isn't easy. It takes experience and learning from ones mistakes in the market. This more skeptical frame-of-mind has certainly improved my investment performance as there's less blowups in my portfolio over time.   The short sellers Marc Cohodes, Carson Block, and Andrew Left can offer some good insights. However, as I've stated before, I have never shorted a stock, as I can only make 100% or less on any shorts, whereas a long idea can bag me 5x, 10x, 50x returns if do my homework, am lucky, and patient.

✪ CHAPTER 7 ✪
SMALL COMPANIES; BIG DREAMS – FUTURE 60 MICROCAP STOCKS

When I was younger, age 18 – 25, I would usually pass on the smaller companies (sub $100M market cap) that popped up on my stock screener. I was fearful of undiscovered micro-cap stocks because of their small size, low institutional ownership, slim trading volume, and little-to-no analyst coverage. It was the fear of the unknown; betting on a tiny company that might fail. I did not want to lose my money on a dumb trade, and look stupid.

However, years of passing on these small companies would later lead to much regret, after seeing some grow from ~ $100M to $1B+ (10x return) in market capitalization, achieving multi-bagger status that I believe most DIY investors pursue in the market. It was a painful phase, and I would repeatedly ask myself: "Why didn't I invest in that stock!? It popped up in my screener, and I conducted extensive independent research. I should have pulled the trigger…"

But I am also a realist, and understand that while all great companies start small, *not all small companies become "great"* (big). Actually, very few small companies get there, or anywhere. For example, the majority of small companies listed on the TSX, and Venture exchange are un-investable, in my opinion, and some companies should have never gone public in the first place; shoddy business models, questionable shell holding companies (zombie stocks), filled with bad actors promoting, pumping, and then dumping garbage. It is actually quite depressing sifting through, and pulling up the charts of most Venture stocks. Countless flameouts.

Therefore, I believe achieving a semblance of success in micro-cap investing comes down to first eliminating the bad batch (80% + stocks) from the micro-cap universe, so that one can focus on the good batch (20% or less) that are meaningful companies with real future prospects, managed by responsible, enterprising owners / operators. Because when companies are at an early-stage in their business life-cycle, you are betting more on the jockey than the horse, hoping that the jockey is not only honest, and able, but executes on his vision, delivering shareholder value.

Here is the thing, though: even if you do pull the trigger and invest in a promising small company, will you have the conviction and wherewithal to hold that stock from $100M to $1B+ market cap? Because successful small stocks do not just shoot up, they are highly volatile (lots of sharp ups and downs in price). Can you stomach watching a small stock drop -20% in a day, rise +10% the next, and then lose 75%+ of its value within the following year? Well, that was part of Amazon's wild ride. Sure, from 1997 – 2017 (20 years), Amazon's stock went up 38,155%, but its trajectory certainly was not linear. Amazon had its IPO in 1997, and started trading at $18/share. MarketWatch succinctly outlined its trials and tribulations over that period: Amazon fell -95% from December 1999 to October 2001 (tech bubble), and fell -64% in 2008 (financial crisis). In fact, Amazon suffered a double-digit drawdown each year since going public and a 20% drawdown in 16 of 20 years. Fun!

Who do you think has owned Amazon since its 1997 IPO? Very few investors bought Amazon's stock at $18, and held until now at $1,849/share (2018). The ones who held Amazon since 1997 were either crazy, genius, or simply forgot to check on their stock portfolio for 20 years. Though they are probably all now relaxing on a beach somewhere. In hindsight, it is interesting to think that most people thought investing in Amazon as recently as even 5-10 years ago was crazy. The majority in 2013 were still doubters, focusing on Amazon's lack of net income, P/E multiple, and continually calling the company grossly "overvalued". Many so-called analysts were claiming that Amazon was overvalued all of the way up until recently when Jeff Bezos finally cracked the list of top 10 richest people in the world. However, it is only now that Bezos is the richest man in the world that most people have realized they missed out on one of the greatest wealth-creating opportunities the world has ever seen. I too am guilty. I should have listened to my non-investor University roommate, who in 2006 said: "Robin, you should really invest in Amazon". My response: "it's overvalued". Doh!

Here is a similar, but Canadian story. In 2007 (age 20), I invested in a small company – SXC Health Solutions

(Healthcare/Pharmacy Technology) – after conducting my own extensive research, and due diligence. Upon investing in SXC Health Solutions, the stock whipsawed so much that I became fearful and sold 100% of my position that same year. I decided to banish SXC Health Solutions from my memory, never to look at, or invest in the company again. Years later, in 2012, it would change its name to Catamaran Corp, and then in 2015, I read in the Wall Street Journal that UnitedHealth Group had announced it was going to acquire Catamaran Corp. for $12.8 billion. I subsequently took a long walk around the block to cool off. Had I not sold my position in SXC Health Solutions, I would have generated multi-bagger returns in my portfolio.

This was not the only case where I had invested in a small stock, and then later sold it out of fear. In addition, I cannot count how many 'errors of omission' (not buying the stock after extensive research) I have committed throughout my DIY investing journey. I have many regrets, which is why since age 25, I plant seeds and water the trees, or in other words; invest small amounts in micro-caps that intrigue me, and then invest more into the winners over time (average up). For example, Tweed.

In my book, *Market Masters*, I wrote in its 50+ page conclusion that I had invested in Tweed, a small cannabis company at the time. The year was 2015, before marijuana became the hot sector. Tweed was trading at ~$1.50/share, and years later would become "Canopy Growth Corp", *the* leader in the Marijuana industry. Canopy Growth Corp now trades at ~$65/share. Owning Tweed was not easy. Though I certainly learned from my past mistakes, and didn't repeat them. Tweed was a dead stock for about one year, and then soared on the marijuana legalization tailwind after the Liberals, led by Justin Trudeau, won the federal election. The stock then soared again following the announcement that Constellation Brands had invested (10% stake) in the company. However, throughout that time, Tweed / Canopy Growth incurred wild swings up and down. The stock did not shoot straight up, and had many doubters. Investing in Canopy Growth early on and achieving a multi-bagger has certainly driven my pursuit of discovering more small companies with lots of upside potential. I might never top that 40-bagger, but I will certainly not fail to try. It is all about discovering new opportunities. Here's my process:

My Discovery Process for Finding Small Companies:

Once per quarter (every 3 months), I will scour all of the companies on SEDAR (official site that provides access to most public securities documents and information filed by issuers with the thirteen provincial and territorial securities regulatory authorities ((“Canadian Securities Administrators” or “CSA”)) and look for new issuers, as well as new quarterly reports from existing companies. I will skip over every single resource, oil & gas, and mining, company. I only invest in Technology, Consumer Products / Services, and 'Diversified Industries'. These three industry groups are less cyclical, and more predictable than other industries. I like to use SEDAR, as stock filters and screeners might eliminate worthwhile small companies from my view. Also, years of poring over thousands of financial statements on SEDAR builds an intuition-like skill in the future, whereby promising companies will start to jump off the screen at you.

In quarterly reports, I look for high revenue growth,

positive cash flow from operations, low levels of debt, and positive net income. However, I will still shortlist a small company that is not generating income but has a path to profitability. My biggest focus for small companies (<= $100M market cap) is high sustainable revenue growth (Quarter YoY, Annual YoY, and 3-5 Year CAGR), fueled by new contracts, accretive acquisitions, penetration into new markets, and / or expanding unit volume. I will also use the official TMX (Toronto Stock Exchange) stock-listing inventories as reference to help guide me through my discovery process. I will access TMX's Technology, and Diversified Industries (includes Consumer Products / Services) pages, and download each inventory (excel file). Altogether, there are ~750 stocks in this initial universe (as at July, 2018).

Stock screeners still play a role in my discovery process, especially to focus on metrics like market cap (<= $100M), revenue growth, cash flow yields, etc. I use the TMX stock screener, as I believe it is the most accurate for Canadian stock data, but in addition, I have used screeners on Stockwatch, and Yahoo Finance, as well as Finviz for U.S. stocks. However, I cannot stress enough that DIY investors should scour all companies on SEDAR, as screeners might miss some stocks.

Finally, I will check the predefined scans on StockCharts.com every day (Monday through Friday) after 4:00pm (market close). What interests me are the stocks making new 52-week highs, and / or stocks trading on higher-than-average volume. This gets me thinking that something interesting might be going on, and so I search further into the possible catalysts via press releases, etc.

At this point, I have started to build a watch list of small Canadian companies (sub $100M market cap), and will exit the discovery phase and enter the next phase: research, and due diligence. I will dig separately into each one of these companies as much as possible, identifying factors that can lead to breakouts, and sustainable growth. Multiple sources of information aid me in this research process, including company websites (investor relations), Stockhouse.com (Bullboard forum), Twitter (there's lots of great micro-cap investors tweeting about small companies, and sharing research), and searches online (Google), which lead to press releases, and sometimes blog posts on these small companies. Also, I'll use *Google Alerts*, as it's an automated way for me to stay up-to-date on companies.

I also like to see whether any respectable micro and small-cap funds / private investors hold these stocks in their portfolios. I will check on Gerry Wimmer's Investorfile, Mawer's New Canada Fund, and Pender's Small Cap Opportunities Fund, among others. Further, while management access would be ideal, unfortunately, most DIY investors cannot just pick up the phone and call the CEO. Therefore, in the past I have attended annual shareholder meetings, and have dialed into quarterly calls. I also try to find any Management interviews on YouTube.

Finally, if there is a storefront that I can visit (e.g. Organic Garage), I will make the outing to a location and explore the store – *Peter Lynch style*.

Throughout my research process, there are certain qualities in these small company stocks that help me determine whether I move them from my watch list to my potential buy list. Below I share my qualification process in the form of questions.

Questions I ask Myself to Qualify Small Companies:

- What are the products / services; does this company offer something new / unique to the market? Is there new technology? Would anyone be unhappy if this company went out of business? Would I use their products / services? Is there lasting utility / appeal?

- Who is running the company – owner / operator or installed CEO? Is there a bold vision for the company? What is the CEO's track-record in leading other public companies, and executing on a vision? What is management's stake in the company (i.e., insider ownership %)? Is management overpaying themselves (as a percentage of revenue)?

- How big is the addressable market? Can the company scale to expand and fulfill demand for its products / services domestically and globally? Can it achieve profitable growth? How easy will it be to acquire, and on-board new customers?

- What is the business model; are revenues repeatable and recurring (e.g. SaaS subscriptions), or inconsistent, and cyclical (e.g. gas tank manufacturers)? Are profit margins good; how will they improve? Is the company structure, workforce and sales / marketing group in place for the company to succeed?

- Is the company vulnerable to business cycles? What would happen in a recession? Does the company have ample net-cash on hand so they are not vulnerable to economic down-cycles? Can growth be funded through its own operations? What is the capital structure?

- Does management have a focused acquisition plan? Have they successfully integrated complimentary companies? Is the industry in which they operate fragmented, and if so is there an opportunity for this company to consolidate smaller companies?

- Are there positive tailwinds? Are tailwinds anticipated in the future (e.g. eldercare)?

- What is the regulatory environment; can regulations dampen the company's growth? Conversely, can regulation bolster company growth? (e.g. Cannabis industry)

- Does the company have sufficient cost controls in place? Are costs eating into profit?

- Will the company innovate; what is the culture? What is the current Research and Development spend (note: R&D is more important for Technology companies)? Does the company plan to expand its product / service selection?

- Can the company achieve a competitive advantage (moat), and fend off any competition? If there is competition, is there room for multiple players? Does the company own any intellectual property? What are the switching costs; is moving to a competitor easy?

- Who is promoting, and supporting the company? Is it under-followed by analysts, and under-owned by institutions? What is the daily / weekly share volume?

- Can a Chinese (or other low-cost) competitor simply produce these goods / services cheaper, or does this company have a following (brand), or a better way of making the product / delivering the service? Can a bigger company (e.g. Amazon) catch on to this opportunity and easily steal market share away?

- Is the stock price validating the company's positive developments, and quarterly releases (e.g. +25% Q1 YoY Revenue)? Does the stock have positive momentum?

- Does the company have any prominent short sellers shorting the stock (e.g. Marc Cohodes, Andrew Left, Carson Block, etc.)? If so, do you believe the short-thesis? Have you considered worst-case scenarios for the company?

- Finally, can this company grow 3x bigger (e.g. $100M to $300M market cap) in 3-5 years? Will the high sales growth continue for years to come? Can the company attract a shareholder base; large investors and institutions that can take the company to the next level? If I'm buying a stock under $5, there's a lot of institutions and funds that won't even buy it under $10. It's only once it hits those higher price levels that they can buy in. In simple economics of supply and demand, all of a sudden there's more demand but supply doesn't change; it's constant. And that pushes the stock up further.

Ultimately, I invest in small companies that pass most of

my qualification questions (above). Because I allocate small chunks of capital to these micro-cap stocks at the onset, I have the wherewithal to hold through volatile swings in the market. After planting these seeds, I will water the stocks that grow (i.e., average up), and hold the stocks that I still have conviction in.

I would like to share with you my current Universe of Small Companies ($63M avg. market cap as at July, 2018) listed on the Canadian TSX, and TSX/Venture exchanges. There are 60 small stocks on my list. I have applied both my discovery, and qualification processes to arrive at these 60 small companies, and will continue to track them in my newsletter. However, this does not mean that I recommend any of these stocks. My list of 60 stocks will change over time. One might find some new ideas below, and then conduct their own research / due diligence.

I have also included some interesting recent information (as at July, 2018) below on a subset of these under-followed companies. While these company developments will be dated by the time you read this book, and most likely already priced into the stocks, it's important to highlight that corporate developments and news like these can push small stocks to new levels. Why? Simply because if analysts aren't covering these companies and conducting any research, most of these developments aren't priced into stocks efficiently (in time and magnitude). You – the enterprising DIY investor – can conduct that research and get ahead of the big, slow institutions.

AnalytixInsight (ALY): On May 16th, entered into a distribution agreement with Thomson Reuters (TSX:TRI) whereby Thomson Reuters will distribute financial research reports created by AnalytixInsight's artificial intelligence platform to customers on Eikon and Thomson One.

Axion Ventures (AXV): On July 3rd, announced the commercial launch of the Company's self-title, 'Rising Fire' in China through Tencent's 'WeGame'. Axion expects Tencent to distribute Rising Fire in a staged manner to approximately 1.5 million active WeGame users immediately, 15 million users by mid-July, and up to 100 million users by mid-August.

GreenPower Motor Company (GPV): On June 5th, announced that it received an order for 100 buses from Creative Bus Sales, the U.S.'s largest bus dealer for sales, parts and service. This 100 bus order represents its largest order to date.

Kraken Robotics (PNG): On July 5th, re-affirmed the Company's 2018 revenue target of over $7 million, which represents at least a doubling of 2017's reported revenue.

Organic Garage (OG): On June 29th, reported its first quarterly positive cash flow from operations and a 38% increase in revenue. Its Liberty Village location is on track to open in fall 2018. On July 11th, announced that its sixth location will be in the central Toronto area.

Symbility Solutions (SY): On May 8th, announced it had completed a definitive agreement to sell its Symbility Health Division business to TELUS Health (CA$16.5 million), allowing the company to apply greater focus to its core Property and Casualty insurance platform while contemplating further transformative M&A with the proceeds of the sale.

WELL Health Technologies (WELL): Chairman & CEO, Hamed Shahbazi previously founded TIO Networks

(TSXV:TNC), a multi-channel payment solution provider specializing in bill payment and other financial services. TIO Networks was acquired by PayPal (Nasdaq: PYPL) for CAD$304 million (Jul 2017).

Wow Unlimited (WOW.A): Michael Hirsh, CEO, co-founded Nelvana Limited (known for Babar, Tintin, Berenstain Bears, Care Bears, and Magic School Bus, etc.). Nelvana was sold to Corus Entertainment in 2000. Later, Hirsh co-led an investment group to start Cookie Jar Entertainment Inc. where he served as CEO until the acquisition by DHX Media in 2012

"Future 60": Small Company Stocks on TSX and TSX/Venture (For Information Purposes Only. These stocks are not recommendations)

Company	Ticker
AcuityAds	AT
AgJunction	AJX
AirIQ	IQ
AnalytixInsight	ALY
Avante Logixx	XX
Axion Ventures	AXV
Bevo Agro	BVO
BeWhere Holdings	BEW
Blackline Safety	BLN
BSM Technologies	GPS
Caldwell Partners International	CWL
Ceapro	CZO
Cortex Business Solutions	CBX
CVR Medical	CVM
Diamond Estates Wine & Spirits	DWS

Company	Ticker
Drone Delivery Canada	FLT
Evergreen Gaming	TNA
FLYHT Aerospace Solutions	FLY
Globalive Technology	LIVE
Good Life Networks	GOOD
GoodFood	FOOD
GreenPower Motor Company	GPV
Greenspace Brands	JTR
Hamilton Thorne	HTL
Hempco Food & Fiber	HEMP
Imaflex	IFX
Intrinsyc Technologies	ITC
Kneat.com	KSI
Kraken Robotics	PNG
Legend Power Systems	LPS
Memex	OEE
Namsys	CTZ
Nanotech Security	NTS
Nexoptic Technology	NXO
Opsens	OPS
Organic Garage	OG
Partner Jet	PJT
Patriot One Technologies	PAT
PineTree Capital	PNP
Pioneering Technology	PTE
Posera	PAY
Quarterhill	QTRH
Redishred Capital	KUT
Reliq Health Technologies	RHT

Company	Ticker
RYU Apparel	RYU
Smart Employee Benefits	SEB
Sunora Foods	SNF
Symbility Solutions	SY
Ten Peaks Coffee	TPK
Titan Medical	TMD
Titanium Transportation	TTR
TrackX Holdings	TKX
Trakopolis IoT	TRAK
Vigil Health Solutions	VGL
VisionState	VIS
Vitalhub	VHI
WELL Health Technologies	WELL
Wi2Wi	YTY
Wow Unlimited	WOW.A
Xpel Technologies	DAP.U

"Future 60": Highest Proven Growth (For Information Purposes Only. These stocks are not recommendations)

For curious readers, below is a subset (1/3) of "Future 60" stocks that have all achieved high hurdles, and together generated an average 20% YTD 2018 return (as at July 10, 2018). Here are the hurdles and actual performance:

- \>= 0% Latest Quarter YoY Revenue Growth (Average = 26%)
- \>= 0% Latest Annual YoY Revenue Growth (Average = 39%)
- \>= 0% Last 5-Year Revenue CAGR (Average = 21%)

- \>= 0% Cash Flow Yield (Average = 8.6%)

Company	Ticker	YTD 2018
Xpel Technologies	DAP.U	207%
Organic Garage	OG	63%
Titanium Transportation	TTR	62%
Evergreen Gaming	TNA	35%
Avante Logixx	XX	33%
Symbility Solutions	SY	31%
Partner Jet	PJT	30%
Hamilton Thorne	HTL	19%
Redishred Capital	KUT	18%
Bevo Agro	BVO	10%
Diamond Estates Wine & Spirits	DWS	10%
Caldwell Partners International	CWL	9%
Intrinsyc Technologies	ITC	6%
AirIQ	IQ	3%
Namsys	CTZ	-3%
Ten Peaks Coffee	TPK	-7%
Wi2Wi	YTY	-9%
Cortex Business Solutions	CBX	-11%
Nanotech Security	NTS	-22%
Sunora Foods	SNF	-23%
Quarterhill	QTRH	-40%

I really enjoy finding promising small companies. The enterprising DIY investors' edge is the ability to not only find companies when they are small, but also to invest in them because institutions have restrictions on holding low market-cap stocks in their funds. In addition, there is usually no analyst coverage for sub $100M market-cap stocks. Thus, the micro-cap universe is largely uncharted territory. The delight comes when a small company that you find and invest in grows into a larger one, crossing that chasm from micro-cap, into small-cap, and then maybe into mid-cap and beyond. That is the dream.

While it is rare for any company to grow from $100M to $1B (10x return), and even rarer for it to grow from $100M to $10B (100x return) the process is still fun, in my opinion. Plus, in those rare cases it can be *very* rewarding for DIY investors, when managing a small portfolio (e.g. < $1,000,000). Buffett once said, "The highest rates of return I've ever achieved were in the 1950s. I killed the Dow. You ought to see the numbers. But I was investing peanuts then. It is a huge structural advantage not to have a lot of money. I think I could make you 50% a year on $1 million. No, I know I could. I guarantee that".

✪ CHAPTER 8 ✪

HOW TO FIND TENBAGGERS LIKE TOP GROWTH INVESTORS

L et's take a break from my own investment philosophy and strategies to examine some of the greatest growth investors ever – Peter Lynch, Philip Fisher, William O'Neil, Joel Greenblatt, and Thomas Rowe Price Jr. – as well as some of the growth investors that I interviewed for my national bestselling book, *Market Masters*.

These investors, especially Peter Lynch, all possessed a passion, and insatiable drive to invest in future "tenbagger" stocks (10x returns). "Baggers" was a term popularized by Peter Lynch that now lives on in financial lore, and is very much a part of my vocabulary.

As said earlier, I love re-reading the investment classics. *One up on Wall Street*, by Peter Lynch is the book that had the greatest impact on me early on. On the back cover of the book, it reads: "…You can discover potentially successful companies before professional analysts do. This jump on the experts is what produces 'tenbaggers', the stocks that appreciate tenfold or more and turn an average stock portfolio into a star performer."

Who doesn't want to find tenbaggers? A couple of tenbaggers in your portfolio can help you beat the market year over year. I've been fortunate to have invested in some stocks that appreciated tenfold ($1,000 turns into $10,000), and one that appreciated 40x (Canopy Growth Corp) but I'm always looking to bag more. When I interviewed some of Canada's top growth investors – Jason Donville, Martin Braun, and Martin Ferguson – for my book, *Market Masters*, I learned from them how they went about discovering tenbaggers. Here are the commonalities:

- Micro / small / mid-cap stocks
- Low stock prices
- Low / or no dividend yield
- Knowledge-based industries (e.g. technology)
- New products / services
- Intelligent capital allocators
- High growth rate in revenue, book value, and cash flow, and then profit spurts in later years

As an example, hedge fund manager Jason Donville's investment in Constellation Software has turned into a 40-bagger ($1,000 turns into $40,000). There's more examples in my book – *Market Masters*.

But back to Peter Lynch – he ran the Magellan fund at Fidelity from 1977 until 1990. His compound annual return through those 13 years was an astonishing 29.2%. During his tenure at Fidelity, Lynch would invest in more than a hundred "tenbagger" stocks, including Fannie Mae, Ford Motors, Philip Morris International, Taco Bell, Dunkin' Donuts, L'Eggs, and General Electric, among many others. But just how did Peter Lynch find those tenbaggers? He offers some hints in his book, *One up on Wall Street* (which I encourage you to read as soon as you're done this book)*:*

"These are among my favorite investments: small, aggressive new enterprises that grow at 20 to 25 percent a year. If you choose wisely, this is the land of the 10- to 40-baggers, and even the 200-baggers.... A fast-growing company doesn't necessarily have to belong to a fast-growing industry. All it needs is the room to expand within a slow growing industry." (p.108; One Up on Wall Street)

"The best place to begin looking for the [fast grower] is close to home — if not in the backyard, then down at the shopping mall and, especially, wherever you happen to work." (p.83)

"There's plenty of risk in fast growers, especially in the younger companies that tend to be overzealous and under financed. When an under financed company has headaches, it usually ends up in Chapter 11.... I look for the ones that have good balance sheets and are making substantial profits." (p.109)

"There are three phases to a growth company's life: the start-up phase, during which it works out the kinks in the basic business; the rapid expansion phase, during which it moves into new markets; and the mature phase, also known as the saturation phase, when it begins to prepare for the fact that there's no easy way to continue to expand. Each of these phases may last several years. The first phase is the riskiest for the investor, because the success of the enterprise isn't yet established. The second phase [i.e., rapid expansion phase] is the safest, and also where the most money is made, because the company is growing simply by duplicating its successful formula. The third

phase is the most problematic, because the company runs into its limitations. Other ways must be found to increase earnings. As you periodically recheck the stock, you'll want to determine whether the company seems to be moving from one phase into another." (p.223-4)

"Selling an outstanding fast grower because its stock seems slightly overpriced is a losing technique." (p.293)

"Wall Street does not look kindly on fast growers that run out of stamina and turn into slow growers, and when that happens, the stocks are beaten down accordingly.... The trick is figuring out when they'll stop growing, and how much to pay for the growth." (p. 109)

That last point, "How much to pay for the growth", is an important one. Peter Lynch suggested a method to judge the price and valuation one pays for growth: Price/Earnings to Growth Ratio (PEG). Lynch said: "the P/E ratio of any company that's fairly priced will equal its growth rate".

Here's how to calculate the PEG Ratio:

PEG Ratio = Price-to-Earnings Ratio (P/E) / Annual Earnings-Per-Share (EPS) Growth Rate.

According to Lynch, a lower PEG ratio is "better" (cheaper), a higher ratio is "worse" (expensive), and a "fairly valued" company would have a PEG ratio = 1.

While Lynch popularized "tenbaggers", publicly explaining his methods to find them – in books, speeches, and interviews – there's other notable growth investors who graced DIY investors with their investing strategies: Philip Fisher, William O'Neil, Joel Greenblatt, and Thomas Rowe Price Jr.. I've included their core growth investing tips below for you to study, and implement later:

Philip Fisher
The 15 Points to Look for in a Common Stock:

1. Does the company have products or services with sufficient market potential to make possible a sizeable increase in sales for at least several years?

2. Does the management have a determination to continue to develop products or processes that will still further increase total sales potential when the growth potential of currently attractive product lines have largely been exploited?

3. How effective are the company's research and development efforts in relation to its size?

4. Does the company have an above-average sales organization?

5. Does the company have a worthwhile profit margin?

6. What is the company doing to maintain or improve profit margins?

7. Does the company have outstanding labor and personnel relations?

8. Does the company have outstanding executive relations?

9. Does the company have depth to its management?

10. How good are the company's cost analysis and accounting controls?

11. Are there other aspects of the business somewhat peculiar to the industry involved that will give the investor important clues as to how the company will be in relation to its competition?

12. Does the company have a short-range or long-range outlook in regard to profits?

13. In the foreseeable future, will the growth of the company require sufficient financing so that the large number of shares then outstanding will largely cancel existing shareholders' benefit from this anticipated growth?

14. Does the management talk freely to investors about its affairs when things are going well and "clam up" when troubles or disappointments occur?

15. Does the company have a management of unquestioned integrity?

Source: Common Stocks and Uncommon Profits. Philip Fisher. © All Rights Reserved.

William O'Neil

CAN SLIM® System:

C stands for Current Earnings. Per share, current earnings should be up to 25%. Additionally, if earnings are accelerating in recent quarters, this is a positive prognostic sign.

A stands for Annual Earnings, which should be up 25% or more in each of the last three years. Annual returns on equity should be 17% or more.

N stands for New Product or Service, which refers to the idea that a company should have a new basic idea that fuels the earnings growth seen in the first two parts of the mnemonic. This product is what allows the stock to emerge from a proper chart pattern of its past earnings to allow it to continue to grow and achieve a new high for pricing. A notable [past] example of this is Apple Computer's iPod.

S stands for Supply and Demand. An index of a stock's demand can be seen by the trading volume of the stock, particularly during price increases.

L stands for Leader. O'Neil suggests buying "the leading stock in a leading industry". This somewhat qualitative measurement can be more objectively measured by the Relative Price Strength Rating (RPSR) of the stock, an index designed to measure the price of stock over the past 12 months in comparison to the rest of the market based on the S&P 500 or the TSX over a set period of time.

I stands for Institutional Sponsorship, which refers to the ownership of the stock by mutual funds, particularly in recent quarters. A quantitative measure here is the Accumulation/Distribution Rating, which is a gauge of mutual fund activity in a particular stock.

M stands for Market Direction, which is categorized into three – Market in Confirmed Uptrend, Market Uptrend Under Pressure, and Market in Correction. The S&P 500 and NASDAQ are studied to determine the market direction. During the time of investment, O'Neil prefers investing during times of definite uptrends of these indexes, as three out of four stocks tend to follow the general market pattern.

Source: How to Make Money in Stocks. William O'Neil. © All Rights Reserved.

Joel Greenblatt
Magic Formula:

1. Establish a minimum market capitalization (usually greater than $50 million)
2. Exclude utility and financial stocks
3. Exclude foreign companies (American Depositary Receipts)

4. Determine company's earnings yield = EBIT / enterprise value

5. Determine company's return on capital = EBIT / (net fixed assets + working capital)

6. Rank all companies above chosen market capitalization by highest earnings yield and highest return on capital (ranked as percentages)

7. Invest in 20–30 highest ranked companies, accumulating 2–3 positions per month over a 12-month period

8. Re-balance portfolio once per year, selling losers one week before the year-mark and winners one week after the year mark

9. Continue over a long-term (5–10+ year) period

Source: The Little Book that Beats the Market. Joel Greenblatt © All Rights Reserved.

Thomas Rowe Price Jr.

His Thoughts from Money Masters on Great Companies:

1. Superior research to develop products and markets

2. A lack of cutthroat competition

3. A comparative immunity from government regulation

4. Low total labor costs, but well-paid employees

5. At least a 10% return on invested capital, sustained high profit margins, and a superior growth of earnings per share

Source: The Money Masters. John Train on Thomas Rowe Price Jr. © All Rights Reserved.

✪ CHAPTER 9 ✪
HOW I MANAGE MY STOCK PORTFOLIO

Picking stocks gets easier over time. But picking stocks and managing a portfolio are two very different things. Managing a portfolio is important, and becomes crucially important as your portfolio grows.

When I opened my first brokerage account at 18, I honestly didn't know what the heck I was doing, but I knew that I needed skin in the game to learn the ropes. Here's what happened with my 5-stock portfolio within the first year: three stocks traded around the same range, one stock got bought out, and the other stock was a high flyer. I got lucky that first year. The following years had their ups and downs; winners and losers. It wasn't until I had invested in the market for 10 years that I truly felt confident in my stock-picking abilities.

Still, today not every stock I pick is a winner. That's impossible. What I've learned is that that cutting my losses and re-allocating that capital into winners will make up for those losses and then some over time. That's basic housekeeping now. But what's really important is how I structure, and manage my portfolio. I believe I've setup my portfolio to best capture any, and all opportunities in the stock market that I am aware about.

I structure my portfolio into these three buckets:

- Mispriced Large Caps (that still have growth)
- Speculative Takeovers
- Small / Mid-Cap Capital Compounders

Mispriced Large Caps (that still have growth)

Notice that I call these "mispriced", and not "value" stocks. The latter ("value") I avoid like the plague, and some examples over time have included: Sears, Blockbuster, Nokia, among many others that are now in the stock market graveyard. With more experience, one can improve their ability to spot larger growth stocks that are nearing the maturity stage of their business life cycle, but that still have growth, as they are making investments for the future. This challenging inflection point – from maturity to transformation, and new highs – is an achievement that only some large companies will make in our generation, and sets the "mispriced" stocks apart from the "value" stocks.

For example, I started loading up on Starbucks' stock in 2008 at around $15/share, when Starbucks was oversaturating themselves in the market, and with most "experts" doubting their strategy of selling high-priced coffee, especially with the financial crisis looming. Not only that, but there were new entrants in the coffee business, such as McDonalds. However, when I bought Starbucks' stock after a big decline (-40%), I never witnessed a drop in traffic among the Starbucks locations near me. Starbucks had clear competitive advantage. I thought, "If Starbucks goes out of business, that's probably when the world will end". Also, I pondered whether business people would ever switch their coffee meetings from Starbucks to McDonalds. Surely, they wouldn't be able to tolerate all those noisy kids. Both companies – McDonald's and Starbucks – are mutually exclusive, meaning they can co-exist without eating into each other's' profits, which most "experts" overlooked at the time. Starbucks' founder, Howard Shultz, would also return to run the company, making new investments for future growth, which would send Starbucks' stock surging upwards for years to come. Starbucks avoided a complete stall in its business, and returned to its growth roots.

Bill Ackman, an activist investor who buys stakes in companies to bring them back onto their growth trajectory, said in my book, *Market Masters*: "with most of our investments we're investing in a great business that has perhaps gotten a bloated cost structure, or that has not thought about its business correctly and maybe over-invested in parts of the business or has not allocated capital correctly, or perhaps has lost focus and owns assets it should sell." I'm looking for those same mispriced large cap opportunities (that still have growth) as Bill Ackman. About a year after meeting Ackman, he acquired a sizeable stake in Chipotle, which stumbled on news that some of its locations had served food with E.coli. The news sent Chipotle's stock into freefall, and I believe it had lost around 40% of its value at one point from peak to trough. But Ackman understood the popularity of Chipotle. There's' constantly line-ups to buy both their burritos and burrito bowls in North America. Chipotle is certainly no

Taco Bell, which is on a systemic decline across North America. Let's face it; Taco Bell food isn't good. Chipotle is now back on its growth track, after that short-term misstep, and the stock has shot back up.

An example of one of my more recent investments into a mispriced large-cap (that still has growth) is Nintendo. Nintendo has long been a video-gaming powerhouse. I'm still a big fan and I'm 31 (maybe I should finally grow up?). But its stock lost 80% of its value from 2007 to 2015. The Nintendo Wii was a big hit but then Nintendo seemed to fall out of favour from there. It started to look like Nintendo would share the same fate as Sega. But then in 2015, Nintendo's management made several key announcements, with plans to unlock their Intellectual Property (IP) – Nintendo Theme Park at Universal Resorts, Mobile Games (partnership with DeNA), and talks of movies, virtual reality, and more merchandising. This was big news in 2015 because Nintendo's management had always been apprehensive to open its IP, and venture into new markets. That's why I initiated my position in the stock in 2015. Nintendo has a treasure chest of valuable IP, which I would compare to Disney's; let's see it continue to open up into new markets, and venture around the world. I'm up 100% on Nintendo since 2015. You can read more about Nintendo's IP plans on their website (Investor Relations).

Speculative Takeovers

As you now know, I invest in micro-caps (sub $100M market cap), which can also be considered "speculative takeovers". Why? Over time, these micro-caps will drop from my portfolio, as they get taken over by larger companies for a premium price. Takeovers, "buy-outs", whatever you want to call them, are especially prevalent in Canada – where small companies are in the scope of much larger, and multinational American companies just across the border. These big companies are looking to expand their market share and get a bang for their (USD) buck.

But it's not just micro-caps that get taken over. I'm always staying on top of merger and acquisition activity ("consolidation") across the three core industries in my focus; Consumer, Technology, and Diversified Industries (e.g. Media). Lately it was the consolidation activity within the Grocery and Pharmacy market in Canada – with Metro's acquisition of Jean Coutu, and before that Loblaw's' acquisition of Shoppers Drug Mart. It was a retail consolidation play to cross-sell through a shared customer base – pharmacy stores. In both cases, I owned and profited from the smaller companies that got gobbled up – Shoppers Drug Mart and Jean Coutu.

Consolidation has also recently happened in the home hardware market. Lowe's, a big American competitor to industry leader, Home Depot, made a bid for Canadian hardware company Rona to expand its presence in Canada. The deal fell through largely because of Quebec intervention, and Rona's stock dropped from its high price that assumed the takeover would go-through, to a much lower level. After the drop, I initiated a positon in Rona, and just sat on the position. I speculated that Lowe's, or another company (maybe Home Depot), would eventually scoop up Rona, with both the Quebec Government, and shareholder's approval this time around.

When Lowe's came back years later to bid on Rona a

second time, it won approval to buy them out, sending Rona's stock up ~100% in one day on the basis of Lowe's juicy premium buy-out offer. Well worth the wait.

The key to successfully investing in speculative takeovers, though, is to only initiate a position if you believe in the company, and would hold your position even if the company doesn't get bought out. It should be a company that, like Shoppers Drug Mart, can generate high returns for you over the long run as an independent company. Though, it's definitely bittersweet when good companies get bought out by larger ones, as you must then find other equally good companies to replace the takeovers.

Before moving on, here's a tip that I learned from my investment in Rona: while I bagged a nice return on Lowe's second buy-out offer, Rona's stock dropped after the first attempt when news released that Lowe's offer was rejected. Usually when news is released that Company A is buying Company B, Company B will move up to right below the announced purchase price, leaving maybe a 5-10% spread; sometimes more, sometimes less. That spread will close once the acquisition is approved, and the sale actually goes through. Thus, I'll sell Company B before that time, taking my profits, just in case the sale doesn't go through.

Small / Mid-Cap Capital Compounders

Last, but certainly not least is the Small / Mid-Cap Capital Compounders bucket in my portfolio. Why? Well, that should be obvious by now. These Capital Compounders are some of the best-performing stocks in the stock market, growing at high rates of return on the foundation of their business models, manager's exceptional ability to allocate capital and operate the business, as well as execute on the company's vision. Stocks like Constellation Software, Savaria, and Tucows in Canada, and Rollins, Accenture, and National Beverages in the U.S., to name just a few examples.

Here's the key financial metrics that I analyze in these 'Capital Compounder' stocks:

- High Growth in Revenue
- High Return on Equity (ROE) / Return on Capital (ROIC), with >= 20% ROE and >= 10% ROIC, with higher hurdle rates for American companies
- Growth in Free Cash Flow Per Share
- Growth in Book Value Per Share
- Growth in Earnings Per Share

I analyze these metrics in a company over a period of at least 5 years as some companies can post a great record in one, or two years, only to then fizzle out years later. That's why a combination of viable business model, non-cyclical industry, and durable competitive advantage is so important because all these factors together determine a company's future. Numbers are just that – numbers, and don't mean anything in the long run, as they are all based in the past. I focus on the business, which is why my favourite sectors to invest in are Consumer, Technology, and Diversified.

Take a look at the screenshots below, sourced from Morningstar.com, which show key financials and profitability metrics for a company that clearly demonstrates outstanding 'Capital Compounder' characteristics over time. But most importantly, it's a company that's built on a strong business model, with an incredibly capable capital allocator and operator at its helm. I'll keep this company a mystery in this example, as it's not about the company – but rather the characteristics that you should seek out in other companies.

Financials — Export — Ascending

	2007-04	2008-04	2009-04	2010-04	2011-04	2012-04	2013-04	2014-04	2015-04	2016-04	TTM
Revenue USD Mil	12,088	15,370	15,781	16,439	18,950	22,980	35,543	37,962	34,530	34,144	33,585
Gross Margin %	16.6	14.5	15.4	15.9	14.8	12.9	13.0	13.1	15.3	17.8	18.4
Operating Income USD Mil	358	3,419	405	442	503	580	839	1,034	1,320	1,669	1,729
Operating Margin %	3.0	22.2	2.6	2.7	2.7	2.5	2.4	2.7	3.8	4.9	5.1
Net Income USD Mil	196	189	254	302	369	458	572	811	929	1,194	1,220
Earnings Per Share USD	0.31	0.31	0.43	0.53	0.65	0.83	1.02	1.43	1.63	2.10	2.15
Dividends USD	0.03	0.04	0.04	0.05	0.05	0.09	0.10	0.11	0.15	0.19	0.20
Payout Ratio % *	10.3	13.7	9.5	8.6	8.3	11.1	10.2	7.6	8.8	8.6	9.4
Shares Mil	625	619	592	566	565	551	561	565	569	569	569
Book Value Per Share * USD	2.09	2.11	2.81	2.94	3.19	3.97	5.79	7.22	8.39	10.47	12.13
Operating Cash Flow USD Mil	403	360	503	491	618	763	1,161	1,429	1,715	1,888	1,901
Cap Spending USD Mil	-373	-280	-238	-231	-225	-317	-537	-529	-635	-906	-949
Free Cash Flow USD Mil	30	80	265	259	394	447	624	899	1,080	982	952
Free Cash Flow Per Share * USD	0.05	0.13	0.53	0.46	0.73	0.80	0.81	2.08	2.12	1.84	—
Working Capital USD Mil	-29	83	56	148	266	-229	143	552	292	229	—

* Indicates calendar year-end data information

Profitability	2007-04	2008-04	2009-04	2010-04	2011-04	2012-04	2013-04	2014-04	2015-04	2016-04	TTM
Tax Rate %	31.74	26.49	31.12	26.52	24.81	24.23	11.43	14.18	24.70	25.03	25.89
Net Margin %	1.62	1.23	1.61	1.84	1.95	1.99	1.61	2.14	2.70	3.50	3.63
Asset Turnover (Average)	4.47	4.83	4.80	4.73	4.93	5.44	4.74	3.60	3.23	2.95	2.84
Return on Assets %	7.23	5.95	7.72	8.71	9.62	10.83	7.64	7.69	8.72	10.31	10.31
Financial Leverage (Average)	2.66	2.65	2.46	2.29	2.07	2.05	3.28	3.26	2.78	2.44	2.37
Return on Equity %	18.53	15.78	19.68	20.60	20.85	22.26	21.25	22.60	23.75	26.71	25.78
Return on Invested Capital %	13.05	11.14	13.39	14.66	16.18	17.60	13.59	13.43	14.72	17.06	16.95
Interest Coverage	—	—	10.06	13.45	18.64	51.32	7.81	9.98	15.25	16.58	16.64

Source: Morningstar.com

There's only a handful of money managers who focus their investing mandate on small, and mid-cap Capital Compounders. Francois Rochon is one of them. Rochon is the founder of Giverny Capital, and I like to call him the "Compounding Machine". I strongly encourage you to read a couple of his investment letters that you can easily find online. If you enjoy the first three letters – read them all!

Rochon's story is definitely inspiring. It's similar to famed investor Francis Chou's story, as his hedge fund started out as a small investment club with just family and friends' money. Rochon's Giverny Capital was officially established in 1998. It's located in Montreal, Quebec, with

$500M+ in Assets Under Management (AUM). Rochon's investment philosophy is centered on "owning outstanding companies for the long term", which means that Francois selects, and invests in Capital Compounders, just like me. See a list of Giverny Capital's latest 13F holdings on Whale Wisdom to learn more about the individual stocks that he currently owns.

The Rochon Global Portfolio has achieved a 15.9% compound annual return since inception, clearly beating the market. That means $100,000 invested in 1993 with Rochon would have compounded into over $3,180,000 by the end of 2016, and even more since then. Yes – Francois is a Compounding Machine. Here are Francois' key points on successful investing, that he included in the Giverny Capital Annual Letter (2016):

- We believe that over the long run, stocks are the best class of investments

- It is futile to predict when it will be the best time to begin buying (or selling) stocks

- A stock return will eventually echo the increase in per share intrinsic value of the underlying company (usually linked to the return on equity)

- We choose companies that have high (and sustainable) margins and high returns on equity, good long term prospects and are managed by brilliant, honest, dedicated and altruistic people

- Once a company has been selected for its exceptional qualities, a realistic valuation of its intrinsic value has to be approximately assessed

- The stock market is dominated by participants that

perceive stocks as casino chips

- With that knowledge, we can then sometimes buy great businesses well below their intrinsic values
- There can be quite some time before the market recognizes the true value of our companies. But if we're right on the business, we will eventually be right on the stock

Now you know that I segment my portfolio into three buckets (with average % allocations) – Mispriced Large Caps (that still have growth) (10%), Speculative Takeovers (10%), and my favourite – Small / Mid-cap Capital Compounders (80%). These three buckets deliver outperformance for my portfolio; ~15% compound annual return. This is what growth investing is all about – allocating capital to the best opportunities, and beating the market over the long run.

CHAPTER 10

HOW THIS HEDGE FUND ACHIEVED A 24% COMPOUND RETURN

You have read about some of the best growth investors ever in an earlier chapter – Peter Lynch, Philip Fisher, William O'Neil, and others. But they're not all actively investing in the stock market anymore, at least not in a professional capacity (Philip Fisher has since passed away). That's why it's important to learn about some of the best growth investors today, who are still actively investing in the stock market. There's always new lessons to learn.

I have a couple of growth investors in mind for the sequel to *Market Masters*. Francois Rochon, being one, as his fund has achieved a 16% compound annual return since inception. Another investor that I would like to interview is Andrew Brenton of Turtle Creek Asset Management. Mr. Brenton will be the focus of this chapter.

Since Turtle Creek was founded by Andrew Brenton on November 1st, 1998, an investment of $1,000 has grown to over $50,000, which equates to a ~24% compound annual return (and 50-bagger status!). That demonstrates a remarkable ability by Andrew Breton to pick winning stocks over the long run. Turtle Creek is long only (meaning they don't short stocks), comprised of North American equities (primarily Canadian, but their U.S. exposure has grown over the years) and has about 25 holdings at any given time, with average market capitalizations of around $7 billion (mid-cap segment).

While I still need to meet Andrew Brenton to document in detail Turtle Creek's investment philosophy and strategies, I have conducted some preliminary research online. Below I've included for you excerpts from Andrew Brenton's "Identifying the Companies We Want to Own (and Their Common Characteristics)", sourced from Turtle Creek's 2015 Letter to Shareholders:

"The universe of companies from which to choose is quite large – there are approximately 2,400 companies listed on North American stock exchanges with market capitalizations of between $1 billion and $25 billion. So how do we sort through them to identify the ones that deserve our attention?

The first common characteristic is that our companies are cash flow positive and the second, related characteristic is that they typically have strong balance sheets. Essentially, none of our companies need us – they don't need the public markets to pursue their business strategy. That doesn't mean they never access the capital markets by selling treasury shares; many of them have issued equity over the years, but they generally don't 'need' to and tend to do so only at attractive prices... Great businesses typically generate more free cash flow than they can profitably reinvest and therefore don't need to raise additional equity capital. More importantly, they don't need to raise equity capital at times when prices would be dilutive to shareholder value. Our companies are good at allocating capital, including the substantial cash flow that they generate.

*In addition to deploying their cash internally on high return opportunities, many of our companies deploy capital externally on acquisitions. This is **the third** common characteristic. Currently, over two thirds of the portfolio, by value, is comprised of companies where growth through acquisitions is an important part of their strategy. Our background and experience allow us to select good acquirers, avoiding the multitude of companies that destroy shareholder value with acquisitions. Our companies have a variety of approaches to creating value through acquisitions but all are capable and disciplined buyers that are not willing to overpay. Our companies would rather sit on the sidelines when prices are too high.*

*A **fourth** common characteristic is returning capital to shareholders, either via dividends or repurchasing their own shares. But in the case of share buybacks, the purpose is not "interesting E.P.S. accretion" as one CEO put it; our companies decide whether or not to repurchase their stock with the same hard-nosed evaluation to which they subject potential acquisitions. Good allocators of capital understand when their shares are cheap, just as they understand when an acquisition is well priced.*

***The fifth** and final characteristic is that our companies have big, rational ambitions. While most of our companies have global ambitions, some are content to operate only* *within Canada or the United States. That's why the modifier 'rational' is important. It's not enough to own companies that have big growth plans. Growth for its own sake can be a recipe for disaster. It's important to own companies that press their advantage when it serves and know when to pull back in the face of a poor environment or irrational competitors."*

To summarize, the companies that Andrew Brenton wants to own have these five common characteristics:

1. Cash flow positive
2. Strong balance sheets
3. Deploy capital externally on acquisitions
4. Return capital to shareholders, either via dividends or repurchasing their own shares
5. Big, rational ambitions

Open Text Corp. is a core holding in Turtle Creek's Fund. I encourage you to read Andrew Brenton's thought process on investing in Open Text. It's a great case study that you can apply to your own stock selection process. You can find the Open Text case study on their website.

✪ CHAPTER 11 ✪

100+ BAGGERS – TOP 30 SUPER STOCKS OF THE PAST 30 YEARS

Throughout this book, I've written extensively about investing in growth stocks and finding those exceptional Capital Compounders in the stock market. I gave the example of Canadian hedge fund manager, Jason Donville's investment in Constellation Software, which turned into a 40-bagger ($1,000 into $40,000), when its stock went from $25/share to $1,000/share, and also my multi-bagger: Canopy Growth Corp. Time will tell whether either of these stocks can crack 100+ bagger status. But what about the actual 100+ baggers? (9,900% + cumulative returns). In this chapter, I'll share the top 30 stocks from the past 30 years on the U.S. market. But first – a story.

I was at the Toronto Reference Library one weekend in the summer of 2017, finally locating the original version (1972) of the investment classic, "100 to 1 in the Stock Market" by Thomas W. Phelps. It's the ONLY original copy remaining in Toronto's public library circulation. I had to make a special request at the library to retrieve it from their archives. If you haven't figured it out already,

I'm a big book nerd. Anyway, the author, Thomas W. Phelps uncovered 365 stocks that turned into 100-baggers, within the 1932 – 1971 period, and explained how one could find the next 100-baggers where each $1 invested grows to $100 or more. I've included below the "four categories of stocks that have turned in 100-to-one performance records", as explained by Thomas W. Phelps in the book's chapter, *Where to Look for the Big Winners*:

- *Advance primarily due to recovery from extremely depressed prices at bottom of greatest bear market in American history. Special panic or distress situations at other times belong to this group too*

- *Advance primarily due to change in supply-demand ratio for a basic commodity, reflected in a sharply higher commodity price*

- *Advance primarily due to great leverage in capital structure in long periods of expanding business and inflation*

- *Advance primarily due to the arithmetical result of re-investing earnings at substantially higher than average rates of return on invested capital*

Phelps influenced top investors today like Chuck Akre, especially on the fourth category above. Below is what Akre said about Thomas W. Phelps' book, "100 to 1 in the Stock Market", and his own journey in the famous speech – *An Investor's Odyssey: The Search for Outstanding Investments*. Akre spoke at the 8th Annual Value Investor Conference in April 2011 (Omaha, Nebraska), right before the annual shareholder meeting for Berkshire Hathaway:

"In 1972, I read a book that was reviewed in Barron's…

*called "101 to 1 in the Stock Market" by Thomas Phelps.
He represented an analysis of investments gaining 101
times one's starting price. Phelps was a Boston investment
manager of no particular reputation, as far as I know, but
he certainly was on to something which he outlined in this
book. Reading the book really helped me focus on the issue
of compounding capital... Here was Phelps talking about
100-baggers, so what's the deal? Well Phelps laid out a
series of examples where an investor would in fact have
made 100 times his money. Further he laid out some of the
characteristics which would compound these investments.
So in addition to absorbing Phelps' thesis, I've been
reading the Berkshire Hathaway (BRK.A)(BRK.B) annual
reports since I've made my first purchase in 1977, so this
collective experience moved me along to a point where I've
developed my own list of critical insights and ingredients
for successful investment."*

It's Phelps' fourth category – stocks that "advance
primarily due to the arithmetical result of re-investing
earnings at substantially higher than average rates of return
on invested capital" that me, Chuck Akre, and other
investors look for in the market to this day. It's only a
select group of stocks that have gone onto generate vast
amounts of wealth for their shareholders, achieving 100+
bagger status.

Let's take a look at some recent 100 baggers. What I'm
about to share with you are the "Top 30 Super Stocks of the
Past 30 Years", originally appearing in the Wall Street
Journal (2016). All 30 stocks achieved 100+ bagger status.
Among them; Apple, Nike, and Home Depot, as well as
other companies that you might, or might not recognize.

Some of these 100+ bagger stocks might surprise you.

Top 30 Super Stocks of the Past 30 Years (*WSJ, 2016*)

Company name	Cumulative total return (%)	Average annual total return (%)
Balchem Corporation	107,099	26.18
Home Depot	67,795	24.27
Amgen	62,850	23.96
NIKE, Class B	42,111	22.32
UnitedHealth Group Incorporated	40,503	22.16
Danaher Corporation	39,526	22.06
Altair	39,070	22.01
Kansas City Southern	37,384	21.83
Jack Henry & Associates	36,716	21.76
Apple	31,428	21.13
Altria Group	28,432	20.72
Paychex	26,838	20.49
HollyFrontier Corporation	26,249	20.4
Monster Beverage Corporation	25,323	20.26
Stryker Corporation	21,329	19.57
Expeditors International of Washington	20,127	19.34
Gentex Corporation	19,095	19.13
CVB Financial	16,232	18.49
Helen of Troy Limited	16,057	18.45
St. Jude Medical	15,951	18.42
Medtronic Plc	15,820	18.39
Raymond James Financial	14,588	18.07
Applied Materials	14,082	17.93
Cracker Barrel Old Country Store	13,912	17.88
Graco	13,593	17.79
SEI Investments Company	13,256	17.69
Precision Castparts	13,152	17.66
Lowe's Companies	13,030	17.62
Watsco	12,176	17.36
Dynamic Materials Corporation	11,943	17.28

Sources: WSJ. FactSet; Windhorse Capital Management

At first I found it amazing that Home Depot (#2 position) achieved a total cumulative return of 67,795% (24.3% compound annual return) because it's a big-box retailer – and the retail industry can be tough. But it makes sense, as Home Depot is incredibly well-run with high return on capital, benefitting from the long-term growth in North America's residential housing market. Plus, new family formation is now picking up again with the advent of the millennial generation entering adulthood, and starting new lives within their new homes.

Remember, that while these "super stocks" are now all mature large-cap companies, at one point in time they were micro/small/mid cap stocks. The question is, which stocks today will be the top performing stocks in the next 30 years? I'm always hunting for 100+ baggers, and so should you. "Plant seeds, and water the trees", as I've said before. Be diligent in your research (turn over as money rocks as possible), place your bets, and then have the patience, and wherewithal to hold small companies through their growing pains, and volatile swings in the stock market.

✪ CHAPTER 12 ✪
SMALL CAP IDEAS - INTERVIEW WITH A PRIVATE TECH INVESTOR

During my talk at the Fairfax Financial Shareholder's Dinner (2017) on "Capital Compounders", I said that I loved "finding capital compounders; those stocks in the small-cap and mid-cap space that eventually grow into large-caps, on the foundation of their exceptional wealth creating ability, fueled by expanding book value per share, earnings per share, and free cash flow per share…the challenge, though, is finding these capital compounders when they're small."

Indeed, searching for, and finding exceptional small companies in the stock market, where there's 1000s of stocks, across multiple exchanges in various countries can be incredibly tough. There's little written about micro and small-cap stocks in the media, and they have little-to-no analyst coverage. Plus, buying into small caps can often be perceived as too risky. My philosophy is that successful investing is a combination of foresight, luck, and risk.

I'm always conducting my own primary research – on

company websites, or through press releases, and financial reports – but I also source small cap ideas from other DIY investors that I believe in. Though I don't 'blindly' invest in their ideas as they can be wrong too.

As discussed in "My 72 Rules", I like to validate my ideas, and the growth investors featured in my book, *Market Masters*, are good sources for small cap ideas. But in this chapter I'm going to tell you about the not-so-well-known Gerry Wimmer, from Toronto, Canada, who runs the website, Investorfile, featuring top small-cap tech ideas.

I recently stumbled upon Gerry's Investorfile site (around the year 2016), and was impressed by his investment track record. Since November, 2011, Gerry's top ideas have "produced an average upside of 239% to date with no losers; no stock picks have negative returns; four [now 6] takeovers / privatizations at a premium to stock price; and paid out a combined total of $0.65 per share of dividends".

Here are Gerry's top five share price performers over the past five years (stats recorded on January 2, 2017):

- Questor Technology Inc. (TSXV: QST) +1,215%
- WANTED Technologies Inc. (Takeover) +478%
- RDM Corporation (TSX: RC) +453%
- Intrinsyc Technologies Corp. (TSX: ITC) +246%
- Quorum Information Technologies Inc. (TSXV: QIS) +245%

One third of Gerry's 18 small cap picks became future takeover targets. His latest small cap stock taken over was RDM Corp. Gerry explained, *"Investorfile blog was one of the very first documented opinion providers on the merits* *of investing in the shares of RDM Corporation following its turnaround. Since we first introduced this stock as a small cap value investment opportunity at a price of C$0.88, Deluxe Corp's proposal to acquire RDM Corporation at C$5.45 values this stock at 519% higher. If you include the dividends paid to RDM shareholders during our coverage period, the total investment return rises to 708%."*

Obviously, I wanted to learn more about Gerry's stock picking strategy and process, and to also share my findings with other DIY investors like you, so I called him one day in the spring of 2017. On the phone, Gerry said that his background was working at a boutique investment banking firm as a research associate and then as an employee in investor relations. He put that collective knowledge to use when he started Investorfile in 2011. As a private investor, Gerry is a shareholder in all of the companies that he covers and shares on Investorfile.

So, what's the secret behind Gerry Wimmer's small cap stock-picking success? He shared these key principles with me on the phone (rough notes):

- Limits stock picks to micro-cap / small cap universe
- Non-resource stocks only (many of Gerry's picks are in the Technology sector)
- Stocks have little-to-no institutional ownership / analyst coverage
- Companies are illiquid (not many shares are traded on the stock market)
- Creates a "hot list" and starts accumulating shares when "the time is right"
- Invests in companies "wisely"; employs a value-

driven valuation system, where companies usually have a 6x or lower Enterprise Value – to – EBITDA (EV / EBITDA)

- Current operations must be cash-flow positive or cash-flow break-even
- Percentage of cash per share makes up a significant portion of the stock's total market capitalization
- All of his picks are considered 'growth stocks'
- Companies have very little debt, and lots of cash on hand, so that they're not as vulnerable to economic down-cycles
- Company financials are easy to understand, with most revenues generated in the western world – North America and Europe
- Management doesn't generally have to raise cash as their business growth can be self-funded through operations
- Shares outstanding is usually fewer than 100 million, but he prefers companies with fewer than 50 million shares outstanding
- Companies enjoy recurring revenue from their products and / or services, without much variability year over year
- Patiently accumulates positions in companies over time, three months in most cases, as most stocks are illiquid
- Sells portions of his stake to take profit off the table after a big run-up in the market, or would sell a full position when there's fundamental business change,

or when management has over-leveraged its balance sheet with debt

- Contacts company executives, and asks about: expansion plans, sales strategy, management experience, etc. Likes "boring management". Doesn't like CEOs who worry about the stock price more than the business, or when there's diverging views of the business among management

- He doesn't "swing at everything". Gerry has only invested in 18 top ideas over 6 years, averaging 2-3 picks per year (as at Jan, 2017)

✪ CHAPTER 13 ✪
KNOWING MORE THAN EVERYONE ELSE

As you learned in the previous chapter, a great private investor like Gerry Wimmer prides himself on the fact that he can invest in inefficiently priced small-cap stocks because for the most part they are not covered by institutions or so-called professional analysts. This brings to mind a similar profession; antique buyers. Here's a story about my uncle, the antique buyer, and his experience in the antique market that I'll parallel to the stock market.

My uncle has worked in the antique market for over 25 years. Over that time, he has indulged our family with countless stories about the antiques he has purchased and then sold at profit to people around the world – U.S., Europe, Japan, China – really everywhere, but primarily in those countries where's there's a large wealthy group of collectors, and aficionados. But he also explains that the industry can be tough. The antique market, much like the stock market, has its ups and downs. Though my uncle has still persisted, earning significant returns through multiple cycles. Here's how, and why it matters to you – the DIY investor.

My uncle knows more than other antique buyers, through years of education but mostly experience, sticking to a disciplined buying plan. He does not over-pay for an antique at auction for which he knows nothing about. If he were to overpay, his returns on that antique would suffer, and he could even incur a loss. However, from time to time he comes across a special opportunity; a high-quality, and rare antique, which he knows has eager collectors, and so he will gladly pay a premium. But – *this is that rare opportunity where my uncle is the only one in the room who knows about that antiques' real value.* For example, an antique that can be bought for $299 at an estate sale and then sold for $9,999 on the open market. Just like the growth investor who finds that rare, inefficiently-priced stock on the stock market because it's not covered by institutions or professional analysts (i.e., the value is not fully known), my uncle explains that he can find lots of underpriced antiques because *the antique market is full of amateur antique buyers / sellers.*

The lesson here is that it's beneficial when you know more than everyone else, and that's the key to investing in the stock market; gaining a relative informational edge over all of the other investors. This is easier in the micro, and small-cap space. Always be researching companies, focusing on the industries that you know well, and understand.

✪ CHAPTER 14 ✪

KEYNESIAN BEAUTY CONTEST – PSYCHOLOGY AND BEHAVIOUR

What I haven't really addressed so far throughout this book is the psychology of the stock market. It can get a little crazy out there, and that can wreak havoc on your mind. As legendary trader, Jesse Livermore said: "The human side of every person is the greatest enemy of the average investor".

I was at a party over the Christmas holidays (2016), and made a bet with an acquaintance there who works in the investment industry. I asked him, "What are your top picks for 2017"? He proceeded to list the stocks that he believed would outperform the market. But then I stopped him half-way at "Visa". I said, "I'll bet you that MasterCard will outperform Visa in 2017". Just friendly competition. After all, we were at a party, and drinks were flowing – we were both a bit buzzed to say the least. He replied, "$100 bucks it won't!" So, at the end of 2017, we decided to pull up the respective charts of MasterCard and Visa, comparing total returns (capital appreciation + dividend yield) to determine who won the $100 bet.

I chose MasterCard based on my past research into both companies. Plus, in 2016, MasterCard (+6%) beat Visa (+0.6%) on price performance. But both stocks under-performed the S&P 500 (+9.5%) that same year.

Anyway, at the end of 2017, I won the $100 bet, as MasterCard beat Visa's performance. However, I also pondered why I made my choice in MasterCard. I thought about John Maynard Keynes' writings on the "Keynesian Beauty Contest", where he said:

*"It is not a case of choosing those [faces] that, to the best of one's judgment, are really the prettiest, nor even those that average opinion genuinely thinks the prettiest. We have reached the third degree where we devote our intelligences to **anticipating what average opinion expects the average opinion to be**. And there are some, I believe, who practice the fourth, fifth and higher degrees." (General Theory of Employment, Interest and Money, 1936)*

So, in other words, I thought about exactly why I made that choice, and whether within the framework of Keynes' "Beauty Contest", I should have rather bet on Visa instead of MasterCard. Since then, the psychology behind all of the stocks on my watchlist, and within my portfolio – why I pick *them* over others – has become very important to me. I've brought 'mindfulness' to my process.

Years after Keynes' writings, Robert J. Shiller, Professor of Economics at Yale University, wrote an article in the *New York Times* (2011), further exploring the Keynesian Beauty Contest:

"...in speculative markets... you win not by picking the soundest investment, but by picking the investment that

others, who are playing the same game, will soon bid up higher." Shiller continued by stating:

"When you hear a conversation among professional investors — including those who manage money for big institutions like university endowments and pension funds — it often sounds as if they are engaged in just this kind of guesswork. You wonder how many people are actually basing their decisions on what is taught in business school: calculating an optimal portfolio based on a rational statistical analysis of fundamental economic data."

So, here's the thing: it isn't enough for you to be right about the company, its prospects, and its fundamentals. You must also consider whether others see what you see. Ask yourself, "Will there be demand for this stock?". When it comes to your own psychology and behaviours in the market – it's best to understand why you do things, so that you don't make basic human mistakes on the basis of the fear vs greed emotional cycle. Be mindful of why you feel things about certain stocks. Being a successful investor means removing one's own hindrances. There's lots of literature out there on psychology and behavioural investing, but for me it comes down to understanding a small subset of important behavioural concepts, which I'll discuss here.

Behavioural Investing 101:

Buy High; Sell Low: Investors tend to come into the market after it's already moved up (buy high). Investors then later get to a point of what's called capitulation (sell low), after a market decline, where they just can't take it anymore regardless of actual valuations. They enter and exit the market at the worst possible times.

Confirmation Bias: When you've taken a position and then look for other people who have the same views, because you want to confirm that you are right. (Always conduct your own independent research and make sure it's right, accounting for all public information at the time.)

Hindsight Bias: The inclination, after an event has occurred in the market, to see the event as having been predictable, even if there was little or no objective basis for predicting that event (in other words, stay humble).

Recency Bias: Investors have the expectation that if the market, or a particular stock has generated a 20% return one year, that it will continue to generate 20% returns in the following years (history doesn't always repeat).

Reference Dependence or "Anchoring": The common human tendency to rely too heavily on the first piece of information offered when making decisions. Investors use an initial piece of information to make subsequent judgments, without incorporating new information (in other words, when your initial thesis to buy a company becomes null and void; sell the stock).

Risk Aversion: Investors are predisposed to be risk-averse. We emotionally view a loss as twice as impactful as a gain. So a market sell-off can greatly influence one's thought process, and subsequent (bad) decision (so, fight the urge to sell just because the stock goes down one day).

Stress: Studies have found that during periods of market volatility, the body naturally produces more cortisol levels to combat stress, which also makes us more risk-averse.

Over-Confidence or "Cocky": Investors might get lucky

their first year investing in the stock market, but if they're not prepared, that luck will soon run out. Only humble, and introspective investors generate wealth over the long term. This can be a very lonely, solitary game.

Notable Psychology / Behavioural Investing Books:

- Extraordinary Popular Delusions & the Madness of Crowds by Charles Mackay
- Irrational Exuberance by Robert J. Shiller
- Your Money and Your Brain: How the New Science of Neuroeconomics Can Help Make You Rich by Jason Zweig
- Inside the Investor's Brain: The Power of Mind over Money by Richard L. Peterson
- How We Know What Isn't So by Thomas Gilovich
- Thinking, Fast and Slow by Daniel Kahneman

✪ CHAPTER 15 ✪
MY BIG ERROR OF OMISSION (AND HOW I AVOID REGRETS)

Recently I was thinking about my old part-time job at Best Buy, and how I committed one of the biggest errors of omission in my investing journey. The year was 2005, and I had just finished my exams (1st Year; University of Waterloo). I moved back to Mississauga with my parents for the Christmas holiday break, and resumed for a short couple of weeks my part-time job at the Best Buy store in Oakville.

While I officially worked in the camera department (who buys cameras anymore!?), I would also walk the floor of Best Buy, going in-and-out of all the departments to help other customers. My daily observation was that the new Apple iPod quickly sold out after only a couple of hours once a new shipment came in. Plus, the store would receive countless callers, asking if there were iPods in stock. The iPod was hot, hot, hot.

I was 18, and as mentioned in the first chapter, you will know that I only held 5 stocks in my portfolio at the time. But while I was always seeking and researching new stock ideas, I didn't invest in Apple. The opportunity was literally right there in front of me. Apple had released a big money-making product. Doh! Big error of omission.

In hindsight, investing in Apple (AAPL) was a no-brainer, but looking back at it logically, Apple still hadn't released its super-product – the iPhone – which catapulted the company into the big leagues. I invested in Apple years later, but obviously didn't capture a big chunk of its price appreciation from 2005 – 2013. You live and learn. Now, I like to plant seeds in stocks if I have a strong gut-feeling. But then if things don't work out for the company, the inner-debate becomes, "What's worse; errors of *omission* (I failed to pull the trigger on an eventual winner) or errors of *commission* (I pulled the trigger but then lost money on a loser)"? The conclusion at this point in my journey is that I don't want any "omission" regrets anymore – I'm ok losing money on some stocks, if the others make up for those losses and then some – 5x, 10x, 50x returns.

I certainly didn't commit an error of omission on Canopy Growth Corp (formerly "Tweed"). If you've read my book, *Market Masters (2016)*, you might remember that I wrote about buying into Tweed in the year 2015 when it was trading around $1.50/share. Now Canopy Growth Corp (TSE: WEED) is trading around $65/share. It might soon become my first 50-Bagger (up 50x), and then maybe even a 100-Bagger. We'll see. Anything can happen.

Investing in Tweed, a small-cap stock, was definitely out of character for me in 2015, as previously I had committed myself to only invest in companies with profitable, long-term track records. However, Tweed just seemed like such a sure thing. The company would serve a once-illegal market: marijuana smokers. By becoming a legal, licensed producer and seller of Marijuana, Tweed would almost literally have a license to print money.

Legalization of marijuana would become one of the greatest wealth transfers of my time – from the black market to a small group of large corporations, and unlike the technology bubble in 1995 – 2000, the Marijuana industry was nothing new. It's an industry that already has millions of happy (stoned) customers. Back in 2015, I explained to my friends that it was "the end of prohibition", comparing marijuana legalization to the alcohol industry, which now boasts a handful of large multinational companies, such as Diageo, and Constellation Brands, but once suffered through a period of prohibition too.

Now that the marijuana industry is legal, regulated, and open territory for big companies, it won't just be smoke products that companies produce, market, and sell – companies will invent marijuana infused foods, drinks, pharmaceuticals, vitamins, beauty products, and the list goes on. Soon you'll walk into a bar, and ask for a "tweed and tonic", just like you do a "vodka and Red Bull", or a "rum and coke", if Canopy Growth can execute that vision.

In 2015, I wrote in *Market Masters*: "I believe that Tweed is 'pregnant with possibility' (optionality). If any or all of these following factors play out for Tweed, I think it will be a big winner: a) become the leader in consumer marijuana; b) generate high profit; c) consolidate most of the micro-marijuana companies; d) benefit from increased de-criminalization or legalization of marijuana in Canada; e) potentially get bought out in the future by a multinational company (I'm thinking of cigarette companies that may want to enter this market). If those options don't play out, though, Tweed will go up in smoke. Consider this an experiment in optionality."

In hindsight, I was right about Tweed. But most importantly; I was happy that I did not commit an error of omission (not buying it).

I bought Tweed, a small cap stock, on the basis of an idea, and a conviction; that the marijuana industry was just about to undergo one of the greatest wealth transfers we've seen in this generation – from the black market to large corporations. I even had a couple of heated debates with hedge fund managers in Canada on my controversial stance, at a time when marijuana stocks could still be picked up for $1, $2, $3/share. Those hedge fund managers would argue: "it's not like people are going to start smoking marijuana, or smoke more marijuana after legalization". Sigh. They totally missed the point – it's now a license to print money. Instead of drug dealers making money, big companies would be making all the money selling weed, and transforming the entire industry into a consumer segment. One of the hedge fund managers quipped, "my friend Mike will still buy weed from his dealer". Well that's the biggest mistake; extrapolating one anecdote onto an entire population. I thought, this hedge fund manager probably didn't go through the frustration of trying to find a dealer who actually had weed on a given night, and when they actually did find a dealer with weed supply, hoping he wasn't shady or sold you a bad batch.

In 2015, I also thought about the wealth transfer from Blockbuster to Netflix, when consumers voted with their feet, opting to stay at home to watch movies. Weird example, yes – but it helped me take the plunge into the marijuana industry. Large corporations were the new drug dealers.

Now that it's 2018, and it's been over three years since my investment in Tweed (Canopy Growth Corp), I'm going to make a bold prediction for the future. In 10 years' time, the large marijuana companies will be seen as "defensive, dividend yielding stocks, just as investors see tobacco, and alcohol stocks today. Call me crazy; I'm used to it.

✪ CHAPTER 16 ✪

MY DAILY ROUTINE – HOW I STAY ON TOP OF THE MARKET

I have a daily routine that helps keep me motivated to discover new stocks, and stay on top of the stocks in my portfolio. My routine spans Monday – Friday (when markets are open). On weekends, I prefer to relax and take a breather from any stock research. Though I'm still observing people's buying habits, checking for new store openings, and paying attention around me to gauge the economy and discover new ideas. Sometimes on weekends I'll read a new investment book that's been on my reading-list for some time. But as mentioned at the beginning of this book, I've already read most of the classics, and so these days it's rare for me to add any new books to my roster.

I want to share my routine with you because a) I've been asked over the past couple of years exactly what I do on a daily basis, and b) I believe that any good DIY investor is an active investor – money never sleeps. Markets change. Businesses come and go. New opportunities emerge. Thus, you need to be aware of as much information as possible.

My Daily Routine:

9:30am (Markets Open):

- Load up BNNBloomberg.ca, and CNBC.com in my web and / or mobile phone browser – refresh periodically throughout the day to stay up-to-date with business and market news

- Open the Capital Compounders Club in Facebook, and follow members' conversation (comments), and new posts throughout the day

- Open, and refresh Twitter throughout the day to see what the "fintwit" community is tweeting about – some good insights, and links to news can be found, plus you can build good comradery

10:00am:

- Login to my brokerage account, and scan through my portfolio (it's been 30 minutes since markets opened), focusing on the early movers. If there's any surprise ups / downs, I look into news, or other sources to find out what's going on

- Check my calendar to see if any of my existing stock holdings (e.g. Constellation Software) are releasing their quarterly reports. I'll have already pre-built a calendar based on data from SEC (U.S.), and Sedar (Canada) websites. If its earnings day, I'll visit the company's website (investor relations page) to read the Qx press release, and accompanying financial documents. I like reading press releases, because most of the financial performance from the quarterly report is summarized in bullet points, and with some management commentary. Optional: you can join companies' quarterly conference calls, and / or go to conferencecalltranscripts.org afterwards to read the transcript from the call. *Google Alerts* also helps me to keep track of news on companies that is all delivered directly into my Gmail account on a daily basis, in one neat email

- Listen to new Podcast episodes in the background while working and researching throughout the day
- Visit my favourite investment blogs to see if there's any new content or insights

11:00am – 2:00pm:

- I'll open my Watchlist on Yahoo Finance (web or app), and monitor moves throughout the day. I'll consider whether to move any stocks from my watchlist to buy-list. If ready to buy, I will determine position size, login to my brokerage account and place the trade. But if more research is required before stock(s) go onto my buy-list, I use Morningstar (10 year finance performance table), StockCharts (technical indicators), and company websites (investment report / overview – PDF, quarterly reports), and forums (Stockhouse, etc.) to conduct more due diligence on any company
- Text / message DIY investor friends, asking them if they're looking at any new ideas, or researching new companies. Tip: open one or more group chats with your investor friends in Facebook Messenger or Whatsapp to stay in touch
- Don't forget to eat a big lunch!

2:00pm:

- I'll find out if there's any new company listings (Initial Public Offerings – IPOs), by visiting the websites of the stock exchanges – e.g. TMX – Canada, and NYSE, Nasdaq – U.S., etc. I'll consider tracking any new IPOs on my watchlist, so that further research can be conducted later using the websites above and in the resources section later on in this book

- Initiate a stock screener if it's been a while. Use the screener on TMX (Canadian stocks) or Finviz (U.S. stocks) to filter stocks based on ROIC, Revenue Growth, EPS Growth, etc.

3:00 - 4:00pm:

- Log back into my brokerage account, and scan through my portfolio (the market will close soon), focusing on the day's winners and losers. If there's any surprise ups / downs, I'll look into news, or other sources to identify the root causes (e.g. stock drop coincides with earnings miss). I'll make any buy or sell trades as necessary. If before the market closes, my portfolio has done better than the market (e.g. S&P 500), I'm pretty happy

- Get caught up on any news on BNNBloomberg.ca, CNBC.com and Twitter ("fintwit" community)

- Open Google Now (if you use Android), and browse through tailored news for the day, which is based on past search results of companies, financial news websites, etc.

4:00pm (Markets Close):

- Check the Predefined Scans on StockCharts.com for bullish stocks, specifically these scans: New 52-Week Highs, Strong Volume Gainers, Bullish 50/200-Day Moving Average Crossovers, Bullish MACD Crossovers, and Gap Ups. If I see promising momentum (during the day, and / or over the course of days or weeks), and want to research more into the root causes, I'll add these stocks to my watchlist

- Check Investcom Market Insights for any more data (e.g. top % gainers)

- Log-out of my brokerage account, and close-out of any websites or apps (this is to clear my mind for the day, as the daily routine of a being DIY investor can be incredibly draining)

- Review Google Alerts (daily) email – a compilation of news that Google has sourced from websites based on pre-loaded companies (e.g. Square, Shopify, Paypal, etc.)

- On a quarterly basis, review new 13F filings data on WhaleWisdom for any new holdings of the hedge fund managers that I am following. For example, checking on Bill Ackman's Pershing Square to see if there's any new positions in the fund. This can help in the idea generation process

Remember – tomorrow is a new day. Markets open again at 9:30am sharp (Monday – Friday). Don't ever feel that you're missing out if you don't initiate a new trade *today*. FOMO – "Fear of Missing Out" – can hurt investment returns if you base a purchase on an emotional trigger. Only move stocks from your watchlist to buy-list (and into your account) after rigorous research, and due diligence. Also, don't just sell a stock that's gone down one day. Look into the root cause. Remember: "In the short run, the market is a voting machine but in the long run, it is a weighing machine" – Ben Graham.

CHAPTER 17

MY INTERVIEW WITH JASON DONVILLE – HEDGE FUND MANAGER

This interview has been abridged from the original interview found in my book, Market Masters (2016)

Aside from his phenomenal stock-picking prowess, market-crushing returns, and beaming confidence, Jason is built like a truck, a physical asset that perhaps benefits him on the lacrosse field more than it does in the office at Donville Kent Asset Management (DKAM). An avid field lacrosse player, Jason also personally mentored his two sons in the sport, and currently coaches the Edge Lacrosse elite travel team. With no disrespect, though, I'd wager that Jason scores even higher in his hedge fund than he does on the lacrosse field. To say that Jason's brain trumps his brawn is no small claim, but it is nevertheless true.

DKAM's flagship Capital Ideas Fund has been the envy of Bay Street. Within just seven years, the Capital Ideas Fund has beaten the TSX Composite Index by 350% in cumulative gains. That's 350% in "alpha," or the amount by which Jason's performance exceeded the benchmark index. From 2008 to 2015, the fund achieved a whopping 525% in cumulative gains. That's a 27.9% annualized return since inception. How did Jason not only beat the index but achieve such high alpha? Straight from the Capital Ideas Fund letter:

"Through the application of our focused investment strategy, we search for companies that possess high levels of return on equity, reasonable valuations, and positive share price momentum. Portfolio companies typically have a track record of achieving high returns on equity, and are capable of generating high returns on equity for many years without the addition of significant amounts of equity capital other than that which is being generated internally. These companies are run by strong management teams that have a significant ownership stake in the business."

The return on equity (ROE) metric is crucial to Jason's hedge fund's success. ROE is not just a figure. It's an initial hurdle that a company must pass, Jason's rigorous test (ROE greater or equal to 20%), in order for any security to progress to future stages of analysis. During our interview we discussed everything from Jason's philosophy, to his process and his strategy, along with the unorthodox way Jason entered the investment world — starting in the navy.

Jason has curly gelled-back silver hair and wears thick, round glasses. On the day we met he was dressed down in jeans and a shirt with rolled-up sleeves. Throughout the interview I noticed that Jason's brain sometimes works faster than his mouth. From time to time he needs to rewind after he speaks, as though he can't vocally articulate his thoughts and ideas at the same rate that his brain produces them. His brain is always working at full speed. If his brain was a car, it'd be a Ferrari. Before starting the interview with Jason, I thought, "Jason would be a great guy to have a beer with. He's a guy's guy, on and off the lacrosse field and his hedge fund's trading floor."

Jason Donville (JD) Interview:

Me: How did you get interested in the markets?

JD: I had lots of part-time jobs when I was a kid. I was always fascinated by the stock market. In the mid-1970s the province of Alberta decided to privatize the Alberta Energy Company. Any citizen of the province of Alberta could then subscribe for a hundred shares down at the local bank branch. And my parents did that. Soon we started to receive annual reports in the mail from Alberta Energy. I would track the movement of the share price of Alberta Energy in the paper every day. My parents probably owned $1,000 of stock. So I just found this to be a really fascinating process. But even if you told me when I was 15 that I was going to become a hedge fund manager I would probably be skeptical.

You only focus your investments on growth industries, and new products and services – why is that?

Well, look around. The world is slowing down growth-wise. Most of that is actually explained by demographics. Obviously the lever- aging and de-leveraging of individual balance sheets, government balance sheets, and corporate balance sheets has an impact, too. But the bigger impact is a result of demographics. When I look around I think, "Where does growth come from?"

Let me give you an example. Leon's Furniture. We don't own it but it's a great company. They're not going to sell 15% more chesterfields next year. Because there's no demographic surge to generate that growth. Where the growth of the world is coming from is new product development in knowledge-based industries, whether it's a drug or a software system or a piece of technology that nobody owns. Whereas 99% of us already have chesterfields and maybe 1% of us are going to replace our chesterfield.

At one point in the last 15 years none of us had a smartphone. That was a growth industry — we all bought smartphones over a period of 15 years. Indeed, all of the action is in the knowledge-based industries, though the health care sector has the added benefit of a very attractive demographic profile. So while there's no demographic surge right now for chesterfields, there is a demographic surge for the kinds of things that people in their sixties and seventies need for health reasons.

How do you select stocks for your fund?

We base decisions on adjusted ROE as opposed to stated ROE because the stated ROE doesn't take into account the difference in the dividend policies of all these different companies. Conservatively, banks are going to make a 12% return per year in the market, year after year. And they're going to realize that return in the form of a 4 to 5% dividend yield and a 7 to 8% capital appreciation. So for the average retail investor who wants to own individual stocks, the banks are actually a great deal. Particularly if you're going to hold them for five or ten or fifteen years because our banks are really strong. Their share prices might come down just because of market sentiment but I'm not worried that they're going to be doing any dividend cuts in the future. Again, though, we look for higher return on equity — 20%.

Your main focus is on ROE. However, you've said that while the companies in the TSX have competitive products and services, their ROEs are usually too low for you.

Not usually too low. They are low. If you start your analysis by looking at the companies that have really competitive products, you'll find that they're not really profitable. Why? Because of the capital structure and the capital allocation skills of the company. Let's say that you and I enter a partnership to make a new smartphone. It has a very nice gross margin and even an attractive net profit margin. But we built up massive overhead, too. And that's where the whole capital allocation game becomes really important.

So first we look for companies with ROE greater or equal to 20%. Second, we look for companies in that high-ROE group that are sustainable based on the competitiveness of their products. Third, we assess management's ability to allocate capital at those companies. Once we validate those three things, we typically find companies that we can invest in.

But how do you determine which companies or products will be sustainable in the future?

I'm continuously looking through my database for high-ROE stocks.

So that's any company that has an ROE of 20% or more. Then I look at the source of the ROE. Is it coming from leverage or is it coming from the sale of assets or is it coming from profit margin? Essentially, return on equity can be broken down into three pieces through DuPont analysis. You've got good ROE and bad ROE. We want to make sure that the ROE is good ROE.

Once I've decided that any company is of interest to me, I'll turn them on to my associates and say, "Get me a two-pager." A two-pager is basically a seven-year history of the company's financials. I often say to people, "If you're thinking of investing in two companies and you run the numbers over the last seven years on both companies and you put them side by side, the good company will leap off the page at you." That snapshot is so important in terms of understanding the difference between a good company and an okay or maybe even crappy company. The reason is because you can fake good ROE in one year. But to achieve high ROE seven years in a row is tough. You can show me the numbers and say, "Here, this is the company's seven-year ROE track record," and I'll go, "I don't even know what they do but there's probably a really good company here." Here's a simple way to think about it: let's say there's a company that makes $20 million in profit and has $100 million in equity. Are you following me?

Yeah, that would work out to 20% ROE.

Yeah. At the end of the year, say you make that $20 million. So now the equity goes up to $120 million if management takes that $20 mil- lion of incremental profits and just puts it in the bank. If it's in the bank then they're going to make 1% on that. So the following year the return is still at $20 million just about because 1% interest is almost no interest at all. But now, let's do the math, it's 20 over 120. The next year after that it's 20 over 140. See how fast the ROE comes down to 15%?

So when I see a company that has achieved an ROE of 23, 22, 23, 24, 23, 22, over the past seven years, without even knowing what industry they're in, I go, "Wow! There's something in place here. There's some- thing magical going on here." That's the magic that you're looking for in terms of those long-term sustainable companies. We can do that analysis in under an hour and that tells us whether we should spend more time getting to know a company.

Where do your associates get that long-term financial data?

We just pull it off SEDAR [System for Electronic Document Analysis and Retrieval, a mandatory documents system for Canadian public companies] and put those two pages together on each company. Those two-pagers look like the reports that Buffett used to read at the local library. That's what we create in house. Nobody else does it that way. Though if they do it, it's only on the large-cap stocks.

Buffett used to peruse all of the Value Line reports.

Right, and it's just boom boom boom boom boom. It's just this straight "Give me the financial history of the last seven years."

Okay, that covers how you would determine sustainability. Now what about management? How do you assess the quality of management? You mentioned they must be good capital allocators.

Okay, so there's a whole bunch of stuff. The assessment of management is something that takes place over time. When you meet with management face to face you don't get 10 hours with these guys; you get an hour. For our type of investing we want competitive advantage and then we want capital allocation skills. So most of the questions we ask when we meet face to face with management are focused on those two areas. "What's happening in your environment? Anybody new, or any new upstarts, or anybody thinking of entering your market?" Because the great enemy of a high-ROE company is competition. If management says, "No. We're not aware of anybody who is thinking of entering the market," then that's a great thing.

Then we get a read on their capital allocation skills. Now, capital allocation takes different forms depending on what business or industry the company is in. In a lending environment like Home Capital where they just write mortgages each year, they don't need to acquire anything or buy anything. Through their network they just put out more capital in the form of mortgages. So it's very straight-forward for them to lend more money. In the case of a lot of the most attractive industries, though, and the reason why a lot of these soft- ware companies are so attractive, is that their client relationships are sticky and they're also high-margin. Once you get clients, you never lose them. Well, that's the same for everybody else in their industry. Therefore, by raising sales and promotional expenses they're actually not going to get much more business because the additional business that they're trying to acquire is actually equally sticky. And then they get to a certain point where the owner wants to move on and then big boys acquire them. Because again, just upping sales and promotion to steal away another client in a sticky business doesn't work.

But often you'll hear analysts say, "There's no organic growth." Well, this is not an organic growth story; this is growth through acquisition. MTY Food Group, which is all about fast foods, does acquisitions but they also open up new locations. So once again we look at MTY Food Group, see that their ROE has never gone below 23%, and determine that they're clearly able to take a year's profits and channel it back into the business to keep their ROE at that level. But so many analysts just talk about the organic growth. That's craziness!

Why is just talking about organic growth so crazy?

Think about it. You and I get the rights to buy a McDonald's in down- town Toronto. And after a year we do $3 million in sales. After year two we do $3.3 million in sales and then it just stays at $3.3 million but the profit margin is massive. However, there will be no organic growth any- more. Because once that location is fully up and running it doesn't grow anymore. It just throws off massive cash flow. So saying, "Let's just up the advertising" is just crazy. There's no more growth there. Instead, what we should do is talk McDonald's into giving us a second location. And yet the number of guys that will criticize these quick-serve restaurants for their lack of organic growth is crazy. It doesn't work that way. Just visualize yourself as a guy running a McDonald's franchise. Get those MBA and B-Comm buzzwords out of your head.

Do you exit a position if management's ROE or capital allocation performance declines?

I'll use Solium Capital as an example. When I first moved back to Canada 1999, I met the founders of Solium Capital. There was a guy with the Calgary Flames who was actually working for them as a salesman. Anyway, they were unprofitable but then merged with another company that brought in a whole bunch of really good technology. It has been profitable ever since. We've owned it off and on. I just recently sold out this year because the ROE dipped down to 17%. Regardless, it's a good company. For a lot of guys, 17% ROE is still high enough.

Who is the top capital allocator in Canada?

Mark Leonard [CEO, Constellation Software].

Who else?

Most of the companies we own have people running them that are very good capital allocators. Because if you can keep your ROE over 20% year after year, you almost by definition are a good allocator. But as the company gets larger, capital allocation becomes more a corporate skill, as opposed to an individual skill. For example, one can attribute the capital allocation skills of a small entrepreneurial company like MTY Food Group to the CEO rather than to the management team as a whole.

So I assume that you primarily take on positions in small- and mid-cap companies?

No, we are market cap agnostic. We buy into companies which have market caps over $15 billion. And then we buy into smaller companies with $100-million market caps in some cases. We don't care about market cap. We care about the ROE.

And you only invest in Canadian companies?

Only in Canada. But this approach works anywhere. This isn't unique to Canada. A few guys in Europe looked at my fund. They were either professors or grad students. I don't remember. They wrote to me and said, "It's hard to find companies in Europe that actually meet your criteria." It's true. The high ROEs are just not there. But in Asia it works. I used to do this in Indonesia, and in Singapore, and it worked in both of those markets.

But what if high ROE comes at a high cost? Currently, the Canadian markets' valuations seem overstretched compared to the growth prospects in the country.

Yeah, valuations are quite rich right now. But we also have a risk-free rate that is somewhere between 1% and 0%. Theoretically, when you work through any of the valuation models, and the risk-free rate goes down to 1%, you can justify virtually any multiple. But a lot of analysts will say, "The historical multiple for the market has been 15 times and currently it's at 18 times." Yeah, but interest rates have never been this low in North America — below 1% or at 1% and probably moving lower.

What risk management mechanisms do you have in place if you're wrong on the direction of the market?

We have always been able to go long and short. We short the market.

Our biggest tool for risk mitigation right now though is put options on the TSX. That's an insurance policy. We buy puts out of money so that they are not that expensive. That won't protect me from a 30% correction but it should protect me from a 10% correction. And it doesn't cost me that much.

So, why would you close off the fund to new money? I just saw the announcement this week.

The reason we're closing the fund is fairly straightforward. If you look at people who manage $200 to $300 million they can put up really good numbers. But when they start to manage billions of dollars then that gets really hard in Canada. The market will force you into the large-caps, which is the most liquid part of the market. I don't mind owning large-caps but I don't want to be in the situation where the small- and mid-caps don't move the market. In Canada, the mid-cap segment is probably the most inefficient part of the market. So it's quite simple: I want to outperform more than I want to manage $3 billion. I don't want to be forced into basically owning the TSX 60.

You achieve greater returns in the mid-cap segment of the market — it's inefficient. But there must be other reasons that you outperform the market.

I think we have a better methodological mouse trap. I didn't invent this style of investing. This is Buffett's style of investing. Why has Buffett been able to achieve a 20% return over 50 years? Because he focuses on companies that are growing at 20%. I also think though that measuring growth in terms of return on equity and book value per share is a better methodological way than measuring growth in terms of earnings per share. For example, for 50 years you can look at the Berkshire Hathaway annual reports; and what's on the first page?

There's the comparison between the S&P 500's return and Berkshire Hathaway's book value growth. Side by side.

He doesn't spoon-feed you. But what's he telling you right there on page one is "This is how you do it."

He focused on book value growth.

Right, he said, "Focus on the growth and the book value per share." Book value per share in old accounting terms was referred to as the net worth of the business. If you focus on companies where the net worth of the business is growing at a very steady clip, then the share price chart will take care of itself as long as ROE stays intact.

So, why haven't other money managers done what you've

done to achieve the same high returns?

A friend of mine in New York used to say to me that "Everybody talks Buffett but only a few people do Buffett." So that would be one aspect of it. Unlike mutual fund managers who have concentration limits, we can concentrate holdings in our portfolio. They can't put 12% of their money into their best idea. And honest to god, if I could only put up to 3% in any of my best ideas I think I would still outperform the market. But it wouldn't be as easy as if I could instead put 50% of the fund into my five best ideas. Because if you're a good stock-picker, concentration works in your favour, and if you're not, you should own an ETF [exchange-traded fund] instead. Truthfully, though, if you're going to use concentration and you're not a good stock-picker, you're going to be out of this business pretty quickly.

Have you ever met Buffett?

No, I've been to Omaha but I've never met him because I'm not in love with the man. I love his ideas and the way he thinks, but I'm not a rock star kind of guy who's like, "Oh my god, to shake his hand would mean so much to me." That doesn't mean anything to me at all. Obviously, though, if he was around or he walked into my boardroom I would love to hear him speak. But Berkshire Hathaway's annual report is good enough.

However, a lot of the best stuff that he wrote was 15 years ago. I have a printout of all the Berkshire Hathaway annual reports going back for the last 50 years. A lot of the stuff from the last 10 years has been more about praising people rather than offering insight into his investment process. So a lot of the stuff that's the best about Buffett has actually been packaged and distilled by other writers. The same can be said of Benjamin Graham. People talk glowingly about reading The Intelligent Investor, which I've read a couple of times, but it's dry.

It is dry. Especially the chapters on bonds.

It's not a great read.

And it's long.

Yeah, exactly. People who tell you that "Oh, yeah, The Intelligent Investor is my favourite book" are the same people who tell you that they love jazz but never go to a jazz club. They say it to be hip and cool. But it's not. There's only two chapters in there that I would recommend to our guys to read. But the people who've written about Buffett are fantastic, such as Mary Buffett's Buffettelogy.

I've read Buffettology. It is a fantastic book.

Yeah, so Buffettology is great. If you can get through Snowball, it's great, too. But also the one by the Wall Street Journal guy that was written about a decade earlier: American Capitalist. It's only about 275 pages. But I think Buffettology is probably the best of all the stuff that's been written on Buffett.

Some would argue that Buffett was an activist investor in his early days. Going back to your point that companies in the TSX have fantastic prod- ucts but through bloated overhead or poor capital allocation, their ROE is usually below 20%, have you ever considered becoming an activist hedge fund manager? Go on boards and improve capital allocation and ROE?

Not yet. Maybe that's something down the road. But it's not some- thing that's on my radar screen. In part because we don't buy turn- arounds. It might be because we don't have the muscle. We wouldn't own enough stock to be able to push for a turnaround. I continue to look for great companies that are a fair price as opposed to cheap stocks. And that's what Buffett evolved into as well in his career.

Any final advice?

Yeah, here's my thesis on life. If you want to be a great doctor, don't go ask a guy who's a counsellor how to become a great doctor. Go ask a great doctor how to become a great doctor. If you want to be a great investor, then study the great investors and pick one who fits your style and then master that style. In terms of the way academics would define it, I'm a growth investor. And, actually, so is Buffett. But Buffett doesn't like that title. While a lot of people call him a value investor based on the way academics look at value versus growth, he's definitely not a value investor. He was before he met Munger, but then he became a growth investor.

Anyway, you must also understand your temperament. And the reason I say temperament is that if you're a value investor then you're investing in turnarounds. Therefore, you need to know how bankruptcy works. You've got to have an ability to know how boards can turn a company around. So when you say you're going to be a really great value investor, there's a bunch of skill sets that have to come with that. You need to be able to know that once a company goes into bankruptcy, how much is left over and how does that process work. There are a few guys who are value investors who don't have that skill set.

I have an undergraduate background in economics and political science. A lot of what I do involves Porter five forces. It's about competitive advantage. So if you want to invest like I do and you enjoy competitive advantage and you enjoy microeconomics and stuff like that, then this is a good style. But your style of investing has to fit your personality type. And I think that there's a lot of more negativity in value investing because you're buying companies that are cheap but are problematic. Whereas I'm buying awesome companies and just hoping that they'll be awesome forever. I get to hang out with the really great CEOs all the time as opposed to having argumentative discussions with mediocre CEOs who aren't doing a very good job running their companies.

Jason Donville's Investing Lessons:

1. "You can get the macro thesis right but still not get the [right] stock picks "

2. "If I'm adding to a position or subtracting from a position, I don't want the market to know. Because I don't want people to front-run me"

3. "Where the growth of the world is coming from is new product development in knowledge-based industries. Whereas 99% of us already have chesterfields and maybe 1% of us are going to replace them"

4. "Think about the market as a baseball game. Let's say there's nine innings in the game. We're now six

years into this bull market. You never know until it's over, but we're probably in the seventh or eighth or ninth inning of the baseball game. That's usually a bad time to own financials."

5. "The time to buy financials is after the market's been corrected"

6. "We base decisions on adjusted ROE as opposed to stated ROE because the stated ROE doesn't take into account the difference in the dividend policies."

7. "First we look for companies with ROE greater or equal to 20%. Second, we look for companies in that high-ROE group that are sustainable based on the competitiveness of their products. Third, we assess management's ability to allocate capital at those companies. Once we validate those three things, we typically find companies that we can invest in."

8. "Return on equity can be broken down into three pieces through DuPont analysis. You've got good ROE and bad ROE. We want to make sure that the ROE is good."

9. "You can fake good ROE in one year. But to achieve high ROE seven years in a row is tough. . . So when I see a company that has achieved an ROE of 23, 22, 23, 24, 23, 22, over the past seven years, without even knowing what industry they're in, I go, 'Wow! There's something in place here."

10. "If you're thinking of investing in two companies and you run the numbers over the last seven years on both companies and you put them side by side, the good company will leap off the page at you."

11. "The great enemy of a high-ROE company is competition."

12. "Most of the companies we own have people running them that are very good capital allocators. Because if you can keep your ROE over 20% year after year, you almost by definition are a good allocator."

13. "Our biggest tool for risk mitigation right now is put options. That's an insurance policy. That won't protect me from a 30% correction but it should protect me from a 10% correction."

14. "In Canada, the mid-cap segment is probably the most inefficient part."

15. "Measuring growth in terms of return on equity and book value per share is a better methodological way than measuring growth in terms of earnings per share."

16. "If you focus on companies where the net worth of the business is growing at a very steady clip then the share price chart will take care of itself."

17. "If you're a good stock-picker, concentration works in your favour, and if you're not, you should own an ETF."

18. "We don't buy turnarounds. We wouldn't own enough stock to be able to push for a turn- around."

19. "I continue to look for great companies that are fair price as opposed to cheap."

20. "If you want to be a great investor, then study the great investors and pick one that fits your style and then master that."

21. "Your style of investing has to fit your personality."

22. "I'm buying awesome companies and just hoping that they'll be awesome. I get to hang out with the really great CEOs all the time as opposed to having argumentative discussions with mediocre CEOs who aren't doing a very good job running their companies."

✪ CHAPTER 18 ✪
KEY EVENTS THAT MOVE STOCKS

It's not just corporate earnings from quarterly, and annual reports that move stocks on the market. It's much more than that, as a wide range of corporate developments are always happening in the business world that influence stock prices. It's your job as an enterprising DIY investor to always be in the know, and on the look-out for events and news that move stocks. You can easily have an informational edge in micro-cap, and small cap companies, as there's usually no analyst coverage. You *are* the analyst, always scanning the market for emerging opportunities, as well as impending failures (to stay clear).

The following are 75+ catalysts that move stocks up and down, which I've observed through 13 years in the stock market. Some catalysts aren't so obvious, and thus might not be priced into a stock adequately, or within a short time frame (especially in smaller companies) – allowing you to possibly capitalize on news before others.

Catalysts that Move Stocks (Up and Down):

- Dividend cut, or increase

- Acquisition offer or rumour
- Partnership, or licensing agreement
- Loss of major customer (as % of sales)
- Return, or departure of the founder as CEO
- CEO, or CFO leaves
- New management joins company
- Low priced / low margin competitors enter market
- Listing on U.S. stock exchange (more demand)
- Promotion to senior stock exchange (e.g. TSX Venture to TSX main board)
- Sentiment changes (e.g. fads)
- Added to or removed from ETF (e.g. Vanguard), or index (S&P 500, TSX/60, etc.)
- Lawsuit, and settlement
- Prominent short position
- One trick pony (single product / first to market company gets out-competed by new company or disrupted by new innovation)
- New 10%+ ownership stake by active fund manager
- Subscriber numbers' ramp-up (SaaS)
- Earnings revision
- Earnings surprise (above analysts' expectations)
- Company enters new market
- New product announcements
- Insider buying or selling
- Restructuring / employee layoffs
- CEO tweets

- New analyst coverage (with "Buy" price target)
- Private placement
- Bought deal
- Spin-off
- Stock split, or reverse stock-split
- New share buy-back program
- Significant new contract (customer)
- Number and type of open positions on career page
- New advertisement campaign
- Adoption of new technology
- Weak, or strong guidance
- CEO CNBC appearance, BNN Market Call mention (Canada), or criticism in News
- Making "most innovative" or "best manager" lists
- Credit rating changes
- Bad public relations
- Product or brand appears in movie, or in show
- Positive "Investor Day"
- FDA approvals
- Regulatory changes
- Political pressure
- Product recall
- Disclosure of internal fraud
- Write down of goodwill of acquisition(s)
- Restatement of prior year's earnings
- Change in business model or strategy
- CEO being accused of sexual misconduct

- Death of founder
- SEC or OSC investigation
- Shifting consumer behavior
- Company gets bought out at x valuation, so there's a re-rating of all similar companies' valuation
- Breakthrough product release (e.g. iPod)
- Arrival of activist investors
- Strategic review (e.g. open to takeover)
- New institutional purchases (or increase in existing ownership %)
- Factory closures, or temporary shut downs
- Major cost-cutting "efficiency" program
- Velocity of press releases
- Supplier order increase
- Competitor declares bankruptcy
- Divestiture of non-core assets
- Expansion of production facility
- Acceleration, or deceleration in revenue growth
- Margin changes
- Celebrity endorsement
- Increase in research and development spend
- Tariffs, or trade agreements
- Cyber breach (e.g. passwords, credit cards stolen)
- Delay in financial filing (e.g. Q1 Report)
- Environmental non-compliance
- Safety issues / accidents
- New website launch

✪ CHAPTER 19 ✪
FUTURE PREDICTIONS TO HELP YOU PICK STOCKS

The market is forward-looking, and always has been. Metrics like the Price-to-Earnings multiple (P/E), which take into account a company's *current* earnings, doesn't really mean anything because what you care about as an investor is the company's future – not it's past.

I'm always thinking about the future, and asking questions like: *How are consumers' tastes changing? What emerging, and underdeveloped technology today will changes our lives tomorrow? Which existing companies are innovating for the future, and which new companies are emerging to capitalize on, and shaping the future?*

Some of these predictions below might not ever happen (e.g. smart lenses), but others will – maybe in the next 10 years. What I want to hammer home, though, is that our world is in constant change, and so you should invest in the businesses at the forefront of that change to not only generate new wealth for you – the investor, but also to contribute to the betterment of our society. By investing in stocks, you are a part owner in those businesses.

My Future Predictions:

- The world will be more electric (renewable energy), and less reliant on fossil fuels, which harm the environment

- Robots will replace jobs, and make our lives easier and more productive, but this will also create new opportunities

- People will eat more organic food, as they increasingly become more conscious of what they consume (you are what you eat!)

- We'll eat more synthetic meats, and not be able to taste the difference, e.g. "impossible burger"

- Prepared meal kits, and healthier fast casual (Chipotle) dining options will replace the fast food chains of past (Taco Bell)

- Usage of plastics, or anything that is not biodegradable in packaging will for the most part go away, and be replaced by alternatives

- The pet population (dogs and cats) will increase

- More people will meet their future partners online, and through apps than any other sources (e.g. friends, school, work, etc.)

- Brick and mortar malls will be less about shopping, and more about 'show-rooms', and experiences

- Universities and schools will evolve with the introduction of virtual classrooms, but also mega-companies (Google, Apple, etc.) will render traditional post-secondary education increasingly obsolete as they setup their own schools (think

McDonald's University) and increasingly not require traditional degrees as a prerequisite for employment

- Robots will serve us in restaurants, and will know what we like to eat and drink based on the past
- More will be done inside ones residence and people will go out less than ever before
- More things will be shared in the future – car-sharing, renting out parts of house / condo, etc.
- Receiving packages will be faster with the advent of intelligent drones; imagine a drone landing on your condo balcony, delivering an Amazon package. Police drones will patrol the skies
- Cars, and trucks will drive themselves, and there will be autopilot driverless hover-taxis. These vehicles will truly be 'connected', and will interact with each other to prevent accidents, and almost feel like 2nd homes during long distance travel
- Services and products that cater to the elderly will benefit from the baby boom cohort that enters their senior years over the next couple of decades
- The consumerization of Marijuana will be extended beyond just smoking, and new applications will be discovered in the form of drugs, edibles, vitamins, drinks, and more
- Big tickets items (cars, houses, etc.) will be more easily researched, but then purchased online without a middleman (e.g. dealership), and picked up in digital garages across the country with just an access code

- Blockchain will find meaningful applications within government, business, and in our personal lives (e.g. payment methods, and tracing an E.coli breakout straight back to its source on the farm)

- Cashless transactions will increase, and cash will no longer "be king" one day

- The e-Commerce share of consumer sales will increase, approaching the majority of how people buy things, and services

- More digital security layers will be required as more transactions, and data are housed on servers, and are open to hacks (e.g. visa card theft)

- As people increasingly join the middle class around the world, there will be more demand for travel, and vacation packages, as well as pilots

- More solopreneurs will start businesses, easily selling products and services online without the need for employees, or a shop, or inventory

- Search will increasingly be done over-voice, rather than typing in a search engine, impacting how we are served ads, effecting our shopping behavior

- More available DNA data will help in the research, and discovery of cures for common ailments

- Average age of death in the developed world will extend to 100

- The majority of infrastructure will be owned, and operated by private, rather than public sector

- Software will continue to 'eat the world'

- Public transportation will improve, becoming faster,

and more accessible, meaning less people will own cars in the future. But if you do own a car, you can send it off on its own after work to pick up fares on auto-pilot, earning you money

- Pair-bonding, and marriage will not be social pre-requisites to have children, with the rapid proliferation of feminism, artificial insemination, and 'designer lab babies'. One will be able to shop for preferences in a baby, much like they do for things on Amazon. Weddings will be a thing of the past that we only see in old movies

- Doctor clinic visits will decline as more people video-call in to explain / show their symptoms, receiving a digital prescription from the doctor

- Department stores completely die out

- Physical toys for children are replaced completely by digital alternatives

- Less people will be reading, and instead they'll be listening and watching (think reading paperbacks vs listening to audiobooks)

- People will work for multiple companies at the same time, in an increasingly freelance-style model, from anywhere in the world, and will pick teams

- Industries will consolidate, and will become more like oligopolies than we've ever seen before

- You'll be "texting by thinking", and checking email with your contact lenses, which will also have cameras built in them for taking photos

- Governments will get bigger as less people work; men will increasingly leave the workforce as their standing, and utility in society changes

- People will drink less sugary beverages
- More people will live in condos than houses, and new houses that are built will get smaller
- Wars will be fought by machines, not by people, and maybe not always country vs country. But before that time, soldiers will wear exoskeletons to enhance their battlefield performance
- You'll watch your favourite robot and / or virtual sports stars instead of human athletes play games
- Nanotech clothes will adapt to the weather outside
- All television will become internet-based, and holographic with force feedback and olfactory output. Advertisements will be completely tailored to individuals, using programmatic advertising
- Printed electronics will be embedded on walls, in paper, and all around us – an ever more pervasive bombardment from ads on a daily basis
- Depression becomes rampant
- More drugs (e.g. Cocaine) are legalized, and new drugs are synthesized to help everyone cope with their new realities as life becomes easier to live
- Interplanetary internet will commence
- Special performance pills will enable medically-enhanced workers before the complete proliferation of artificial intelligence and robots transform the workplace as we know it
- You'll be able to communicate with dead relatives, and other people via Virtual Reality (VR), and some

people will rather live within their virtual reality

- The fridge in your kitchen will restock itself, and your entire home will be "smart"

- CGI actors will replace human actors

- You'll finally have access to all of the world's knowledge in one click – everything from the past, and everything the *second* it happens

- Cheaper, more efficient and accessible 3D Printing will print everything from new shirts, to tools that you can use around the house – the cottage industry will be reborn

- Space travel will become as affordable as a round-the-world plane ticket

- Nano-bots will perform medical procedures inside our bodies, and also live within our bloodstream to prevent sickness. Pills will be able to detect cancer, and nurses will be robots

- There will not be any pilots flying planes

- Prosthetic brains will allow for a second life. We'll be able to plug information streams directly into the cortex (think Neo in the Matrix)

CHAPTER 20

MY UNIVERSE OF GROWTH STOCKS – MODEL PORTFOLIOS

These are the growth stocks currently in "my universe", meaning that I've either invested in these companies in my stock portfolio or have them on my watchlist. These are not my recommendations to you (please see the "Disclaimer" at the beginning of this book) but rather a glimpse into the stocks that I short-list based on my research. Things change, and so these companies might not look as promising to you in a couple of years.

My Universe of Growth Stocks (as at October, 2018) –

If you want to stay up-to-date all the time on my Universe of Growth Stocks, you can become a Patreon member for only $5/month. I've partnered with Patreon to host my model growth stock portfolios for you. Give it a try; go to Patreon.com/RobinSpeziale. You can leave anytime you want, but as a Patreon member you'll also receive some freebies from me over time and you'll never miss anything – newsletters, new stocks that I like, and upcoming events. Email me if you want more information on Patreon before you give it a try – r.speziale@gmail.com.

Capital Compounders:
Pollard Banknote (PBL)
Constellation Software (CSU)
Photon Control (PHO)
Logistec (LGT)
TFI International (TFII)
Enghouse Systems (ENGH)
Premium Brands (PBH)
Dollarama (DOL)
Lassonde Industries (LAS)
Stella-Jones (SJ)
Brookfield Asset Management (BAM)
Canadian National Railway (CNR)
Savaria (SIS)
CCL Industries (CCL)
Metro (MRU)
Tucows (TC)
MTY Food Group (MTY)
Gildan Activewear (GIL)
Saputo   (SAP)
New Flyer Industries (NFI)
Stantec (STN)
Alimentation Couche-Tard (ATD)
Richelieu Hardware (RCH)
Computer Modelling Group (CMG)
CRH Medical (CRH)
Spin Master (TOY)
BRP (DOO)

Sylogist (SYZ)

Tecsys   (TCS)

Calian Group (CGY)

Transcontinental (TCL.B)

Sleep Country (ZZZ)

Magna International (MG)

Kinaxis (KXS)

Fairfax India (FIH.U)

CGI Group   (GIB.A)

Great Canadian Gaming (GC)

FirstService (FSV)

CAE (CAE)

Andrew Peller (ADW.B)

Future 60 Small Company Stocks:

AcuityAds (AT)

AgJunction (AJX)

AirIQ (IQ)

AnalytixInsight (ALY)

Avante Logixx (XX)

Axion Ventures (AXV)

Bevo Agro (BVO)

BeWhere Holdings (BEW)

Blackline Safety (BLN)

BSM Technologies (GPS)

Caldwell Partners International (CWL)

Ceapro (CZO)

Cortex Business Solutions (CBX)

CVR Medical (CVM)

Diamond Estates Wine & Spirits (DWS)

Drone Delivery Canada (FLT)

Evergreen Gaming (TNA)

FLYHT Aerospace Solutions (FLY)

Globalive Technology (LIVE)

Good Life Networks (GOOD)

GoodFood (FOOD)

GreenPower Motor Company (GPV)

Greenspace Brands (JTR)

Hamilton Thorne (HTL)

Hempco Food & Fiber (HEMP)

Imaflex (IFX)

Intrinsyc Technologies (ITC)

Kneat.com (KSI)

Kraken Robotics (PNG)

Legend Power Systems (LPS)

Memex (OEE)

Namsys (CTZ)

Nanotech Security (NTS)

Nexoptic Technology (NXO)

Opsens (OPS)

Organic Garage (OG)

Partner Jet (PJT)

Patriot One Technologies (PAT)

PineTree Capital (PNP)

Pioneering Technology (PTE)

Posera (PAY)

Quarterhill (QTRH)

Redishred Capital (KUT)

Reliq Health Technologies (RHT)

RYU Apparel (RYU)

Smart Employee Benefits (SEB)

Sunora Foods (SNF)

Symbility Solutions (SY)

Ten Peaks Coffee (TPK)

Titan Medical (TMD)

Titanium Transportation (TTR)

TrackX Holdings (TKX)

Trakopolis IoT (TRAK)

Vigil Health Solutions (VGL)

VisionState (VIS)

Vitalhub (VHI)

WELL Health Technologies (WELL)

Wi2Wi (YTY)

Wow Unlimited (WOW.A)

Xpel Technologies (DAP.U)

Chinese Technology Stocks (and their U.S. Equivalents):

I obsessively researched Chinese Technology Companies in 2018. Baidu, Alibaba, and Tencent (aka BAT) are widely known in the North American investor community, but these other Chinese technology companies (below) – not as much. I've mapped this list of Chinese Technology Stocks (most are traded on U.S. exchanges - NYSE, NASDAQ – unless otherwise noted below) to their North American equivalent companies (e.g. Alibaba / Amazon)…

Alibaba $BABA / JD $JD / Pinduoduo $PDD (Amazon)

Tencent $TCEHY (Facebook)

Baidu $BIDU / Sogou $SOGO (Google)

IQiyi $IQ (Netflix)

Weibo $WB (Twitter)

BYD $BYDDY / Nio $NIO (Tesla)

Momo $MOMO (Match Group)

YY Inc. $YY / Bilibili $BILI (YouTube)

CTrip $CTRP (Expedia Group & Booking.com)

Baozun $BZUN (Shopify)

Huami $HMI (Fitbit)

51Job $JOBS (Monster Worldwide)

58.com $WUBA (eBay)

Cheetah Mobile $CMCM (Zynga)

NetEase $NTES (Activision Blizzard)

Huya $HUYA (Twitch)

AutoHome $ATHM (CarMax)

Xiamo (Apple)*

IPO: Tencent Music (Spotify)

IPO: Didi Chuxing (Uber)*

IPO: Meituatuan (Uber Eats)*

IPO: Ant Financial (PayPal)*

*Not traded on any U.S. exchanges
IPO = Initial Public Offering (at the time of writing this book, these
companies had still not had their initial public offerings on the market)

15+ Great Canadian Technology Stocks:

Open Text (OTEX)

Constellation Software (CSU)

Shopify (SHOP)
Computer Modelling Group (CMG)
CGI (GIB.A)
Tucows (TC)
Photon Control (PHO)
CAE (CAE)
Ceridian HCM (CDAY)
Descartes Systems (DSG)
People Corporation (PEO)
Sylogist (SYZ)
Tecsys (TCS)
Enghouse Systems (ENGH)
Kinaxis (KXS)
The Stars Group (TSGI)

U.S. Disruptors and Innovators:
Alphabet (GOOGL)
Align Technology (ALGN)
Amazon (AMZN)
Apple (AAPL)
Upwork (UPWK)
DocuSign (DOCU)
Facebook (FB)
Horton Works (HDP)
Hub Spot (HUBS)
Instructure (INST)
Match Group (MTCH)
National Beverage (FIZZ)

Netflix (NFLX)

NVIDIA (NVDA)

Salesforce (CRM)

Service Now (NOW)

Square (SQ)

TelaDoc (TDCO)

Tesla (TSLA)

Twitter (TWTR)

Wayfair (W)

WorkDay (WDAY)

ZenDesk (ZEN)

Carvana (CVNA)

Stich Fix (SFIX)

Altair Engineering (ALTR)

ANGI Homeservices (ANGI)

Intuit (INTU)

Splunk (SPLK)

SailPoint Technologies (SAIL)

Ollie's Bargain Outlet (OLLI)

Smartsheet (SMAR)

Red Hat (RHT)

Proofpoint (PFPT)

Ebix (EBIX)

MongoDB (MDB)

Blackbaud (BLBK)

Simulations Plus (SLP)

iRobot Corporation (IRBT)

Five Below (FIVE)

Masimo Corporation (MASI)

Q2 Holdings (QTWO)

Paylocity Holding Corp (PCTY)

BlackLine (BL)

Intuitive Surgical (ISRG)

Bright Horizons Family Solutions (BFAM)

Fortinet (FTNT)

Paycom Software (PAYC)

Activision Blizzard (ATVI)

The Ultimate Software Group (ULTI)

Atlassian Corporation (TEAM)

Arista Networks (ANET)

Guidewire Software (GWRE)

Vmware (VMW)

Allie Mae (ELLI)

Fonar Corporation (FONR)

Okta (OKTA)

Palo Alto Networks (PANW)

XPO Logistics (XPO)

Check Point Software (CHKP)

2U (TWOU)

Coupa Software (COUP)

Cornerstone OnDemand (CSOD)

Dropbox (DBX)

GrubHub (GRUB)

Turtle Beach Corporation (HEAR)

Cognex Corporation (CGNX)

Etsy (ETSY)

PayPal (PYPL)

Tableau Software (DATA)

Yext (YEXT)

IPG Photonics (IPGP)

Stamps.com (STMP)

Zscaler (ZS)

Ferrari (RACE)

The Trade Desk (TTD)

Carbon Black (CBLK)

Cannabis Products & Services Companies:

Canopy Growth Corp (WEED)

Canopy Rivers (RIV)

CannTrust Holdings (TRST)

Hempco Food and Fiber (HEMP)

Hexo (HEXO)

Hill Street Beverage Co (BEER)

Namaste Technologies (N)

National Access Cannabis (META)

Eve & Co (EVE)

Molson Coors (TAP)

Aleafia Health (ALEF)

The Second Cup (SCU)

Robotics/AI/Automation:

It was legendary hockey player Wayne Gretzky, who said: "Skate to where the puck is going to be, not where it has been". So, over the course of a year, I've been thinking a lot about Robotics/AI/Automation.

We're still at a very early point on this new S-Curve; Robotics/AI/Automation is going to change the way we live, work, and play. It's hard to fathom that now because research and development can be slow at first, and it takes time to commercialize new technology. These are the other major S-Curves of innovation from the past 50 years that have played out; PC, Internet, and Mobile. Some major breakthrough companies were born from these significant eras of innovation, creating vast amounts of wealth for their shareholders. For example, Microsoft (PC), Google (Internet), and Apple (Mobile).

Thinking about the future excited me, so I decided to conduct some research early on in 2018. I recently finished compiling a list of Canadian Robotics/AI/Automation companies that are publicly listed on the TSX, and TSX Venture. These stocks were hard to dig out though. There are over 20 companies in total that I found (see below).

On this list, some are old companies reinventing themselves, and investing in new Robotics/AI/Automation technology, (e.g. BlackBerry), while other companies are new, and launching innovative products / services (e.g. Kraken Robotics). In 2017, these companies were up an average +64%. Not bad, but past results certainly don't indicate future performance. Plus, I'm very doubtful that any of these companies will grow as big as Microsoft, Google, or Apple (wishful thinking!). Though, BlackBerry almost got there on the Mobile S-Curve with their innovative Smartphone, before being dethroned by Apple, and Google's Android – two very tough U.S. competitors.

This exercise of combing through hundreds of stocks on the TSX, and TSX Venture to uncover

Robotics/AI/Automation companies felt a lot like early 2015, when I started researching all of the emerging marijuana stocks (and ultimately investing in Tweed / Canopy Growth Corp, TSE: WEED). However, unlike in the marijuana industry, these Robotics/AI/Automation companies were a lot tougher to unearth, as each have unique technologies. Thus, each company must be examined closer to determine their own specialized technologies, and competitive advantage, etc.

Why did I go through all of this effort in Canada? Well, we don't have a Robotics ETF. And there is very little small / micro-cap technology coverage or research in Canada. Though, look at the U.S.; they have two (2) recently launched ETFs: ROBO (2013) and BOTZ (2016). You can look further into these ETFs, and see all of their holdings, by doing a search on Google. Here are some ideas:

Reliq Health Technologies (CVE:RHT)

WI2WI (CVE:YTY)

Visionstate (CVE:VIS)

Kneat.com (CVE:KSI)

Nexoptic Technology (CVE:NXO)

Axion Ventures (CVE:AXV)

BlackBerry (TSE:BB)

Blackline Safety (CVE:BLN)

BeWhere Holdings (CVE:BEW)

Vigil Health Solutions (CVE:VGL)

Kraken Robotics (CVE:PNG)

Magna International (TSE:MG)

Trakopolis IoT (CVE:TRAK)

Drone Delivery Canada (CVE:FLT)

ATS Automation Tooling Systems (TSE:ATA)

Sierra Wireless (TSE:SW)

Titan Medical (TSE:TMD)

AirIQ (CVE:IQ)

Open Text (TSE:OTEX)

Quarterhill (TSE:QTRH)

NovaTeqni (CVE:NTQ)

FLYHT Aerospace Solutions (CVE:FLY)

Patriot One Technologies (CVE:PAT)

Pioneering Technology (CVE:PTE)

Celestica (TSE:CLS)

Opsens (TSE:OPS)

TrackX Holdings (CVE:TKX)

Intrinsyc Technologies (TSE:ITC)

Memex (CVE:OEE)

CONCLUSION

Thanks for reading *Capital Compounders*. Email me (r.speziale@gmail.com) and tell me what you thought of the book. Don't forget to subscribe to my Investment Newsletter (it's free!) on RobinSpeziale.com/Subscribe so that we can stay in touch in the future and you won't miss anything – new writings, freebies, and get-togethers. Also, I will be very grateful if you review this book on Amazon.

I hope you learned some new ideas on investing in growth stocks, beating the market, and finding future tenbaggers, and 100-baggers. I've done my job if you feel that you have a acquired a better "edge" (informational advantage) to win in the stock market. Anyone can make money in stocks – the market doesn't care, or even know about your race, gender, or sex – it's blind. You can make money in the stock market if you do your research, and wisely pick the right stocks over time. But remember; it's impossible to pick winners 100% of the time, especially when they're still small companies. Stay humble.

In the introduction, I gave the example of buying Amazon's stock in 1997 (IPO), and then having both the conviction and wherewithal to hold the stock through its ups and downs as a public company. Successful growth investing takes a combination of foresight, luck, and risk. You've got to invest in your best ideas, based on all available knowledge that you have at the time. Not all of your stock picks will be winners (and sometimes you'll be surprised in the ones that do make it big!). Most importantly, you won't make any money at all unless you take some risk and actually plant some seeds in small companies rather than sit on the fence and miss out on opportunities. Don't have regrets.

Here's a question for you –

Would you rather:
(A) Lose 100% of $1k?
Or
(B) Make 100% (2x), 300% (4x), 900% (10x) on $1k?

Obviously (B). However, you have to be open to try & fail in order to bag the big ones. Most people will fail to even try in the stock market, because they focus on (A) (loss). Play the probability game. Go multi-bagger hunting.

You only really need 5-10 big multi-baggers throughout your investing journey to have a stellar portfolio:

Multi-bagger	Gain	ROI
2-bagger	100%	2x
3-bagger	200%	3x
4-bagger	300%	4x
5-bagger	400%	5x
10-bagger	900%	10x
100-bagger	9,900%	100x

Don't be discouraged, and don't give up. I've met some people – young and old – who feel the stock market is far "too risky". Sure – it's impossible to make money all the time in the market. Your portfolio might contain 60% winners (stocks that go up). But over the long run, it's proven that stocks have beaten other types of investments – Bonds, GICs, Gold, etc. Your individual performance in the stock market will be good as long as your winners outperform and outnumber your losers.

As I explained in the "My 72 Rules" chapter, "managing a portfolio is like gardening. Instead of watering my weeds [which too many people do], I water my flowers, so that they can grow bigger [seems common sense, but tough in practice]. In other words, I reward my existing holdings (the "winners") by increasing my stake in them when they post great earnings results quarter after quarter". Legendary trader, Jesse Livermore, once said: "As long as a stock is acting right, and the market is right, do not be in a hurry to take profits".

I've also met younger, budding investors (under 23) who will not start investing in the stock market because they don't think they have enough money. I then tell them my story where I started at age 18 with a small amount ($10,000) in my brokerage account, investing in 5 stocks ($2,000 each). Now, my portfolio has grown 50x that initial investment to $500,000, through compound returns, and new capital. My advice: start as soon as you can, no matter how much money you have. Why? Because of the power of *time value of money* and *compounding returns*. So, "Just do it", as the Nike adage encourages. Think about it; even if you just invest $5,000 on an annual basis, starting at age 18 into a portfolio that generates a 10.59% compound annual return (S&P 500 average), by the time you turn 85 your portfolio will be valued at around $50,000,000. I'm not kidding. Clearly, it does not hurt to start young and to start small. Here's a side story: Francis Chou (fund manager) was a 25-year-old repairman for Bell Canada when he pooled $51,000 from himself and six coworkers to start an investment club. That investment club would eventually blossom into Chou Associates Management Inc., which now has around $1 billion of assets under management. Francis is definitely an inspiration as he started small – only $51,000.

Patience is also a virtue. I see too many people become impatient in the stock market. You won't get rich overnight. You need to hold stocks through ups, downs, corrections, recessions, and big crashes (-50%) to build wealth in the stock market. That's what Peter Lynch, one of the greatest investors ever admits is one of his biggest mistakes too, explaining. "selling your winners and holding your losers is like cutting the flowers and watering the weeds". In Forbes' 100th Anniversary Edition, Lynch went on to provide this valuable example: *"I visited the first four Home Depot's ever built. I sold that stock after it tripled, and then it went up another fiftyfold. If you're great in this business you're right six times out of ten. But the times you're right, if you make a triple or ten-bagger, it overcomes your mistakes. So you have to find the big winners. I sold way too early on Home Depot..."*

You'll win at this game if you have both the passion and drive to understand how the market works, and when you are motivated to research as many stocks as you can. It's the only way to know which stocks to pick. Practice makes perfect. But yes – this game can be very lonely, and solitary at times. You'll do well if you start to love the game. I'm always thinking about the stock market – everyday, even when I'm doing other things like vacuuming my condo. Famous speaker, Earl Nightingale, said: "We become what we think about most of the time, and that's the strangest secret", and Napoleon Hill, author of the book, *Think and Grow Rich*, said "Whatever the mind can conceive, and believe, it can achieve". It'll become obvious later that success in the stock market starts in your mind. Believe in yourself, study hard, and then take the plunge. But never stop learning. There's a continual stream of new growth opportunities in the stock market for you.

Here's some new disruptive growth industries, and technologies that I'm thinking about now:

- Healthtech
- Cyber Security
- eGambling
- Consumer Cannabis
- eCommerce 2.0
- Cloud Enterprise
- ElderCare
- AI, Automation, and Robotics
- Programmatic Advertising
- Electric Auto-Pilot Transportation
- Sharing / OnDemand Economy
- 3D Printing
- Virtual Reality
- Blockchain
- New Consumer Products

- Drones
- Organic (and Alternative) Foods
- Cleantech
- Interactive Media
- Genomics
- Wearables
- eSports
- Smart Home

I'm frequently asked what it takes to be a successful investor. Although investing is absolutely not a formulaic process (if it was, it would be *too* easy and I wouldn't have written this book), I've distilled my investment success thus far into ten points. Here they are (this was much harder than I thought):

1. Invest in good quality companies you know, and understand (strong business model is #1)
2. Invest in companies that will grow, and can gain market share anywhere in the world
3. Invest in companies with superb management teams, that have a stake in the business
4. Don't invest in story stocks – think independently
5. Research companies; acquire an informational advantage, read quarterly statements, etc.
6. Use logic; not emotions – and don't become greedy
7. Invest in 25–50 stocks (your best ideas), focusing on smaller companies in emerging industries, with new products / services that will change the world
8. Only invest in a stock if you'd buy the entire company and be happy to own it for 10+ years

9. Invest for the long-term; the tortoise won the race

10. Continually plant new seeds (look for new ideas – but remember that the next Zuckerberg won't invent Facebook, it'll be something completely different), and water the trees, while limiting your losers

Next Steps

Let's keep in touch. Here are some of the ways that we can connect and talk more about investing in stocks. Don't forget to subscribe to my free investment newsletter (there's already 3,500+ subscribers from around the world). Email me at r.speziale@gmail.com or go to RobinSpeziale.com/Subscribe.

- Email me if you want to talk more about investing: r.speziale@gmail.com. I'll reply to you personally

- Meet up for a coffee if you live in Toronto, Canada (or nearby) at a local Starbucks or Tim Horton's

- Visit my website at RobinRSpeziale.com

- Follow me on Twitter @RobinSpeziale

- Watch my YouTube Channel

- Buy my National Bestselling Book, *Market Masters*

- Become a Patreon on Patreon.com/RobinSpeziale

- Post a short review of *Capital Compounders* on Amazon (I'll really appreciate it!)

- Buy the paperback version of this book on Amazon if you haven't already

ADDITIONAL WISDOM FOR YOUNG PEOPLE JUST STARTING

*"How in the hell could a man enjoy being awakened at 8:30 a.m. by an alarm clock, leap out of bed, dress, force-feed, shit, piss, brush teeth and hair, and fight traffic to get to a place where essentially you made lots of money for somebody else and were asked to be grateful for the opportunity to do so?"- **Charles Bukowski***

Most people live their lives thinking that they are in control, but really it's an 'illusion of control'. They go to school, get good grades, and then enter the workforce. They "choose" a profession – whether as an engineer, scientist, or accountant, and in-debt themselves to a big mortgage, two cars, a cottage, and other shiny things. Then for the next 40 years, they work at a job that they don't really like in order to pay for those things that they don't really need. They've become "debt slaves" to the system, and looking back, realize that all of that schooling was a process to merely create productive corporate workers out of them. They voluntarily enlisted themselves into a life of indebtedness. They're lost, and ask themselves, "What's the point in all of this – what have I done with my life?", but only have this epiphany when it's too late.

Well, I'm telling you now; unlearn what you've learned.

The great Mark Twain said: "I never let my schooling interfere with my education" and that "all schools, all colleges, have two great functions: to confer, and to conceal, valuable knowledge."

Unlearn what you've learned.

I wasn't a very good student in school. I got so-so grades, and most of my teachers told me that I was either inconsistent, didn't pay attention to detail, or seemed uninterested in class. Well, they were right. I was uninterested. While I quickly skimmed through my science textbook, I poured over books on investing in the stock market throughout high school, latching onto role models like Warren Buffett, Peter Lynch, and Benjamin Graham as I developed an insatiable drive to make it on my own by investing in stocks. I decided that I didn't just want a "normal" life. I wanted financial freedom so that I could have real control and do something that I actually enjoy.

And so when I entered the University of Waterloo in 2005, I was more excited about the fact that at 18, I could open my first brokerage account and trade stocks, than anything else. Fast forward to today; I built a $500,000 stock portfolio, which I plan to grow to $1,000,000 by 35. And that's not even "work" to me. It's fun. How much fun? Well, on my way to building wealth, I wrote three books on finance & investing, with one becoming a national bestseller; *Market Masters*. I wanted to share the wealth; that is – knowledge on investing in stocks. I was only 28. Oh, and I was rejected by 50 publishers. Not to mention that I don't even have a finance background to even "qualify" me for writing a book on finance. No bachelor's degree in finance. No CSC, no CFA, and no industry experience. Honestly; I'd probably flunk all of those exams, and never fit into the investment industry. But I'm self-taught. I really know how to invest in stocks and build wealth in the stock market. I'm great at it. And here's the secret: I'm great at investing because I love the process. I'm always learning, and I'm always motivated to be better.

So, put down your text books from time to time and actually educate yourself on what YOU want to learn. You've got no excuse today with the proliferation of information on the internet; everything is available at your fingertips. What do YOU want to learn? What excites you? What comes easy to you? Build on that. If you want to be financially free, deliver value to people, feel pride in what you do, and take control of your life. You need to monetize something that you are passionate about. Make your passion your business.

Start with an idea, and then be mindful about how to make it happen. Here's my blueprint for success: mix intelligence, energy, and focus.

Be mindful of all three because you need intelligence, energy, and focus to actually achieve something. Trust me; there's people out there who are intelligent but have no energy, and other people who are full of energy but have no focus. You need all three. And when I say intelligence, I mean learning something of value, and being knowledgeable in something that actually inspires you. Remember what Mr. Twain said: "don't let school interfere with education".

So after reading this, think about what I've said and

unlearn what you've learned. I know; it's tough because you'll be breaking from convention. But I don't think you want to become like everyone else; living your life with an 'illusion of control': go to school, get good grades, and then enter the workforce, working at a job that you don't really like in order to pay for things that you don't really need.

Don't become lost, asking yourself, "What's the point in all of this – what did I do with my life?", and only realizing that until it's too late. Unlearn what you've learned. Educate yourself; learn about something that really interests you. Build something great with your knowledge. Make it your business. Lead a great life. A free life. And take control of you.

BONUS – MY DIY INVESTOR FRIENDS SHARE STRATEGIES

Reverse Engineering the Perfect Stock
By: Paul Andreola, Small Cap Discoveries

We are going to tell you about the perfect stock that could make you millions of dollars. Few investors know about this stock even though it's a multi-bagger in plain sight. Okay, on with it – what is it!? Here are a few clues…

The stock is a micro-cap, under $20 million-dollar market cap, and has had three straight years of operating profits. The company is rapidly growing at over 25% per year, all of it generated organically.

The company has high gross margins at 75% and a scalable business model, allowing operating earnings to grow at a 50% clip.

The company's industry is experiencing secular tailwinds and growth is expected to accelerate over the next few years.

Being a first mover, the company has no competitors in its niche and new entrants have failed to displace this company because of switching costs and the mission-critical nature of its product.

The combination of pricing power and lack of capital requirements allow the company to achieve extraordinary returns on its invested capital, well over 100%. The company is debt-free and funds its growth entirely from operating cash flows.

Insiders collectively own 40% of the company and the CEO has a 25%+ stake. He bought in with his own money 5 years ago and has added to his stake through open market purchases.

Management has maintained a clean share structure consisting of less than 30 million shares outstanding and no warrants or preferred shares. The low float and small size of this company have kept its stock off the radar of institutions, which own less than 10%.

We all know there is no such thing as a "perfect stock." That said, we believe there exists certain characteristics that form the DNA of any investor's dream: a multi-bagger than you can hold on to for years.

What follows is our list of 14 such qualities, organized by key fundamental, business model, and technical criteria (note we use stock/company interchangeably throughout). Enjoy!

Key Fundamental Criteria:

Profitable

Profits are the lifeblood of any company and cash flows generated by the business ultimately determine the value of your investment.

A company that can fund itself internally avoids financing risks, which can cause massive losses through dilution or excess debt. While bio-techs prove positive cash flows are not necessary for success, working with profitable companies will simplify your valuation process and margin of safety assessment.

At a minimum, we will want to see two solidly profitable quarters and preferably a 3-year track record of profits (or more!).

Rapidly Growing

Assuming a company is generating returns on capital above the costs of that capital, growth is enormously beneficial to the company and its shareholders.

New products, customers, and business lines typically bring more profits and drive the company's intrinsic value.

Ideally, all of this growth should be organic. Too often, acquisitions don't deliver on their promised synergies and yield much of their value to the seller through premiums paid. We will want rapid organic revenue growth, a minimum of 25% year-over-year.

Attractive Valuation

The key to investing is not finding the best companies, but rather the largest discrepancies between price and intrinsic value.

Buying at a low valuation provides downside protection in the event your thesis does not play out, while allowing for huge upside if things go well. Valuation is more art than science, and finding the most useful metrics to employ can be tricky.

Our valuations usually begin with an adjusted Enterprise Value/EBIT multiple, which incorporates the company's balance sheet and strips out non-operating items to better present true earnings power.

We will want this multiple below 10 and ideally below 7 – the lower, the better.

No Debt / Financing Requirement

Debt can juice a company's returns but often leaves the business vulnerable to the unexpected: a major customer loss, a regulatory change, or a patent infringement suit.

This situation is made worse when the market knows an equity raise is coming, effectively holding the company hostage to its share price. Investing carries enough risk as it is – crossing off dilution/bankruptcy risk is key to putting the odds in your favor.

Example: A $10 million dollar market cap company has $6M in debt, no cash, earns $2 million dollars a year in EBIT, and trades at 8X Enterprise Value/EBIT.

If the company suffers a major contract loss which cuts EBIT in half, you would face an 80% loss on your investment assuming the company maintains its valuation multiple(1 million X 8 = 8-6 = 2 million).

High leverage magnifies negative events in a big way.

We will want our company to have no debt and plenty of cash in the bank for growth investment. The company should have no need for future debt/equity raises and fund itself entirely through internal cash flows.

Durable Competitive Advantage

Durable competitive advantages, or economic moats as Warren Buffet calls them, are derived from only a handful of sources: brand power, switching costs, patent/government protection, and network effects.

Economic theory holds that in absence of one of these

forces, competitive pressure will reduce all company's Return on Invested Capital (ROIC) to the cost of capital.

Sources of economic moats are not all created equal. Government protection often proves unsustainable and brand power can be just as easily eroded in some cases.

We will want our company to benefit from switching costs, network effects, or both. Banks, software providers, and business service companies are all beneficiaries of switching costs. Social media and auction platforms are prime sources of network effects.

High Returns on Capital / Low Capital Requirements

The less capital investment a company requires to keep its competitive position, the more profits that are left over to invest in growth or be returned to shareholders.

By nature, some companies require little capital while others require seemingly endless amounts to stay afloat.

This intrinsic quality, along with competitive positioning determines the Return on Invested Capital our company can achieve. Return on Invested Capital (ROIC) is a key value driver – the higher the ROIC, the more shareholders stand to benefit from growth.

Example: Capital-light/high-ROIC businesses include software, database, and franchising companies.

Capital-intensive/low-ROIC investments to be avoided include railroad companies, automotive manufacturers, and above all, airlines. By requiring our company to have a ROIC above 50%, we will be big beneficiaries from any growth the company generates.

High Gross Margins

Gross Margin (GM) refers to how much profit is left after the direct costs of products/services are covered. The higher the gross margin, the more profits will accelerate with sales growth.

Example: If Business A has 75% GMs and Business B has 25% GMs, Business A will experience three times the impact on profits from each dollar of new business as compared to Business B.

High gross margin companies include patent licensors, medical device manufacturers, and pharmaceutical companies. Examples of low gross margin companies are automotive suppliers, construction contractors, and retailers.

Gross margins will vary widely based on industry but in general, the higher the better. We will want our company to have gross margins of at least 50%.

Scalable Business Model

Scalability refers to a company's ability to leverage its infrastructure as it grows. A good measure of this is the Degree of Operating Leverage (DOL), or the percent change in EBIT divided by the percent change in revenues.

Example: Once a Software-as-a-Service (SaaS) company invests in the infrastructure to create and sell its software, each incremental subscription can be delivered at virtually no additional cost.

Compare this model to a restaurant, which must pay rent, labor, and food costs with every location opened. Software and database companies are often scalable, while restaurant operators and manufacturers tend not to be.

Ideally, we will want our company's operating expenses

to grow at half the rate of revenues or less (DOL >= 2).

Non-cyclical, Recurring Revenues

Recurring revenues afford a business the advantages of predictable cash flows to base investment decisions on and high lifetime customer values.

Recurring revenues also aid investors in projecting future cash flows and performing valuations.

A stable, non-cyclical business offers the similar advantage of predictable cash flows, while offering safety in case of a sharp economic downturn.

Example: Any business with a subscription model, such as SaaS or security monitoring, is likely to have recurring revenues. Food, tobacco, and alcoholic beverage companies are all classic examples of recession-resistant businesses.

We will want a business with over 50% of their revenues recurring and a low sensitivity to general economic conditions.

Small-cap

Much like large companies forge their own anchors as they grow, small companies have the law of small numbers on their side. Small size often offers a long runway for growth and magnifies each positive development.

Example: Think of a SaaS company doing $10M per year annually that announces a $2M contract. This business becomes 20% more valuable overnight, and perhaps far more given the operating leverage inherent in software.

We will want to stick to companies below a $300M market cap, and ideally less than $50M.

Low Float / Clean Share Structure

Low float (freely tradeable shares) results from a low share count, high inside ownership, or a combination of the two.

From a technical standpoint, a low share float can lead to massive price increases as investors rush to bid on a limited supply of shares.

On a more fundamental level, the float is a reflection of how management has financed the business in the past and their relative ownership of the company.

We will want no more than 50 million shares outstanding and preferably less than 30 million. The float should be significantly lower due to insider ownership (discussed below). We will also want to see a clean share structure, with low or no warrants or exotic convertible instruments.

High Insider Ownership

We want a management team that behaves like owners and this is not possible unless they ARE owners.

For the micro-caps we are interested in, we will want to see insiders collectively owning at least 30% of the company, with the CEO himself owning at least 15%.

It is also important to assess how management got their stakes – did they buy in with their own money or was it given to them through options and share grants?

Management adding to their stakes through open market purchases is often a big plus. This demonstrates insiders believe in the company's future and you should too.

Low Institutional Ownership

For a variety of reasons, many institutions cannot invest

in the small-caps we are interested in. Some have restrictions against stocks under $5 or companies that trade on the Toronto Venture Exchange (TSX V).

With all the desirable qualities discussed thus far, institutions will be drooling over our company waiting for the company's size/liquidity to reach their buying criteria.

When this happens, look out! Triple digit gains are quite likely as institutions pile into a "must own" stock.

To leave this big catalyst open, we will want to see institutional ownership under 10%.

Secular Industry Tailwinds

Never forget to look beyond the fundamental and technical factors to understand the underlying trends in the company's industry.

Beyond a company's own efforts, secular industry tailwinds are often necessary to sustain our 25+% revenue growth target.

Industry tailwinds also have the bonus of attracting investor attention, which can lead to big gains as our company is viewed as a unique play in a hot sector.

Example: Organic foods, mobile applications, and network security software are all industries undergoing secular growth phases.

5 Key Tips to Boost Investment Returns
By: Be Smart Rich (Blog)

There have been many people who have impacted me positively ever since I started managing my own investments in September 2014 – Robert Kiyosaki, Warren Buffett, Peter Lynch, Joel Greenblatt, Stephen Jarislowsky, etc. Through the journey, I had switched my investing styles from mutual funds investing to index investing to dividend growth investing and value investing to finally GARP investing. Thanks to all the people who positively impacted me, I have been able to beat the markets.

One of the people who impacted me positively is Robin Speziale. I got to know Robin about 3 years ago when he published his bestseller *Market Masters*. If you have not read the book, check out his book here as well as his blog. Robin has been doing amazingly well in growing his portfolio and I have no doubt that he will do very well going forward. Robin recently contacted me for content submission that gets to be featured in his sequel of the *Capital Compounders* eBook, so this is dedicated to it.

Developing a Personal Investor's Edge

When you read Peter Lynch's books, he often talks about identifying and developing a personal investor's edge. Almost everyone has an edge. A person who works in an innovative tech company. A person who works in a company that just won a major deal to supply important parts to a much larger company. Or even being a parent who has kids that are so addicted to watching Spin Master's Paw Patrols every day.

My edge? I used to be an auditor and am an accountant,

so I know how to find info and interpret financial statements and know some of accounting tricks that can be pulled off by some companies. I am sure Robin and other investors will share key metrics and ideas for successful investing such as revenue, earnings, cash flow growth, ROE, ROIC, avoiding mining, gold, resources companies, penny stocks etc.... through his book so let me talk about some of the other areas that investors often overlook but certainly help to boost investing performance.

1. CEO Compensation Test

Finding great ethical CEOs is half the battle when it comes to investing (at least for me). If they are ethical, then they will shape every little aspect of running a company towards increasing shareholder value. Google 'SEDAR' with the name of the company and look for a document called "Management Information Circular" (For American investors, you should google EDGAR and look for DEF 14A Proxy Statements) where you can see how much salary the top executives have received in cash, stocks, stock options, bonus, pension and other benefits such as car allowance for the last 3 years.

The below shows MTY Food Group's Management Information Circular.

Name and Principal Position	Year Ended	Salary ($)	Share-based Awards ($)	Option-based Awards ($)	Non-equity Incentive Plan Compensation ($)		Pension Value ($)	All Other Compensation ($)	Total Compensation ($)
					Annual Incentive Plans	Long-term Incentive Plans			
Stanley Ma President, CEO, Chairman and Director	2017	426,785	Nil	Nil	Nil	Nil	Nil	23,414[1]	450,199
	2016	384,689	Nil	Nil	Nil	Nil	Nil	23,414[1]	408,103
	2015	378,462	Nil	Nil	Nil	Nil	Nil	27,260[1]	405,722
Claude St-Pierre COO, Secretary, Director	2017	213,392	Nil	Nil	Nil	Nil	Nil	Nil	213,392
	2016	202,315	Nil	Nil	Nil	Nil	Nil	Nil	202,315
	2015	190,038	Nil	Nil	Nil	Nil	Nil	Nil	190,038
Eric Lefebvre CFO	2017	316,154	Nil	2,938,678[6]	Nil	Nil	Nil	14,227[2]	3,269,059
	2016	276,282	Nil	Nil	Nil	Nil	Nil	4,144[2]	280,426
	2015	237,548	Nil	Nil	Nil	Nil	Nil	3,563[2]	241,111

Considering the company made close to $90M in free cash flow in the 2017 fiscal year, Stanley Ma's $450K is less than 0.5% of that. That's a great indicator that the CEO cares about growing the company than their pay cheque. You see $3M stock options issued to Eric, but you may be interpreting it as ok, as he will be the successor of Stanley Ma this year.

You can of course compare that to other companies in similar industries and size that you may be interested in. For example, Concordia International where the company lost $10M in cash flow in 2017 but the former and current CEO's 2016 salary combined was close to $10M. Its market cap used to be around $3B but it is only $18M now. The company has lost 99.85% of its value in the last 3 years. You know why.

Name and Principal Position	Year	Salary ($)	Share-based awards ($)(1)(2)	Option-based awards ($)(3)	Non-Equity Incentive plan compensation ($)		Pension Value ($)	All other compensation ($)	Total compensation ($)
					Annual Incentive Plan	Long-Term Incentive Plan			
Allan Oberman(4) Chief Executive Officer and a Director	2016	$116,667	$2,103,027	-	-	-	-	$25,000	$2,244,694
	2015	-	-		-	-	-	-	-
	2014	-	-	-	-	-	-	-	-
Mark Thompson(7) Former Chairman and Chief Executive Officer	2016	$683,333	$3,581,783	-	-	-	-	$3,490,451	$7,755,567
	2015	$691,000	$4,430,894	$1,775,031	$2,020,000	-	-	$11,038	$8,927,963
	2014	$446,667	-	-	$185,256	-	-	-	$631,923

If you smell that something stinks, go find better opportunities elsewhere. There are many companies with ethical and competent CEOs that pay themselves reasonable salaries thus everything they do with the company would likely be shareholder oriented.

2. Insiders Ownership Test

The Management Information Circular also shows insiders ownership. I have been always thinking that owner

/ manager's substantial interest of the business they run is extremely important as they are aligned to the interest of the shareholders. But if the ownership is too high, let's say 50-60% then the stock price may get impacted negatively when the insiders want to diversify by selling their ownership through a bought deal offering at a lower price than market price. That happened to Spin Master and Stella Jones recently and the value of the shares dropped to the level of the bought deal offering where a discount had to be given to get the deal closed. Just a temporary downside you need to keep an eye on. You could see it as an opportunity to buy more as long as fundamentals of the company remain intact.

Shareholder Name	Number of Common Shares Held[1]	Percentage of Issued Common Shares[2]
Stanley Ma	4,885,643	19.4%

The circular also shows directors' ages and background and how long they have been working as a director.

You can also see how many options at what prices were given to all insiders. The best of the best but extremely rare founder-run companies don't issue free options or free shares to the insiders because he/she would hate share dilution. When you find companies like that, take a close look and you may want to put some money in if everything else checks out. Compare number of options issued to the insiders to total outstanding number of shares to measure the greed of those insiders.

3. Cash Flow Test

I can't emphasize enough on this. I know several dozen ways of manipulating revenue, net income and expenses. Name a few? Aggressive capitalization of PPE, intangibles, financing fees and others, loose impairment policy of assets combined with aggressive forecasts, less accrual of expenses and liabilities, overstating revenue by recording returns of the inventory as resell revenue, overstating revenue with higher charge-off expenses, overstating revenue by aggressively recognizing deferred revenue etc. I can go on all day.

However, I can only think of a few ways of manipulating cash flows which is simply delaying the expenses and collect aggressively before cutoff date. That being said, it can't be manipulated for more than 1 year.

Businesses do not run on earnings and revenues but on cash flows. So, when net income and revenue look great but actual cash flow looks bad then you have got to throw a red flag and watch it very carefully.

Supplement return on equity and earnings multiples metrics with return on cash flows and cash flow multiples. Cash flow growth is also a very good indicator that the business is doing great.

4. Debt to Free Cash Flow (or Cash Flow) Test

Simple but very effective, when you want to quickly measure the financial health of company. No one can bankrupt the company except creditors with covenants. Just find out how much debt the company has and how long it would take for the company to pay off assuming the company is using 100% of the free cash flow to pay off the debt. MTY's debt was around $220M and its free cash flow was around $90M in 2017 so it would take less than 3 years to pay off. If it is more than 7 years, I would be cautious. If it is more than 10 years, I would stay away in general.

This criterion is extremely important when you look at

turnaround situations. You have got to look for broken stocks and stay away from broken companies when looking at turnaround situations. I have witnessed very closely how high debt load and covenant breaches kill companies. It starts with creditors imposing more cash restrictions then the managers of the creditors are forced to send out very expensive consultants who monitor the company (otherwise the managers would be in trouble). The scavengers mostly think about their own pockets rather than helping the company turnaround. A slow and painful death awaits. So, make sure to test debt to free cash flow when trading or investing in turnaround stocks.

5. Short Test

Like environmental activists balancing out growth-oriented businesses and policies, short sellers balance out the investing community. Listen to well-known short sellers' thesis and think carefully about what they are saying. Often, they do an extreme amount of research, so it would likely be worth it. When well-known short sellers start talking about accounting inconsistency, abrupt departure of CFO or Chief Accounting Officer, you better listen. Accounting scandals end badly most of the time. When something stinks, take your profit or loss and run. Jim Cramer often says, "Bulls make money. Bears make money. Pigs get slaughtered" You don't want to be the pig!

Bonus Content - Dividend Myth Buster

I have seen lots of people and bloggers investing in companies that are heavily leaned towards dividends. I would say if you are around 20-40 then I would put very little to no emphasis into dividend investing. I don't blame you as I was one of them. It blinded me for a while. It probably has been blinding your eyes. Time to open your eyes. If you are investing in companies that are paying more than 50% of earnings or cash flows as dividends, you are missing out on growth. Some companies are just so great in allocating capital and with the scale they have, they can use the money in better ways than paying it out as dividends. Dividends should not have any material impact when it comes to your investing decisions unless you are semi-retired or retired and looking for dividend cheques to supplement your other income streams. I am not saying dividend paying companies aren't great investments but just saying there are so many other important metrics that people are missing out on if they are fixated on dividends.

At the end of the day, what really counts is not how many dividends you have received but how much total returns you have made during the year. If you have been fixated on dividend investing, it's time to compare your total returns, including dividends, to the returns of the ETFs that you could alternatively invest to. After all, investing in well diversified ETFs is relatively cheap and takes no effort at all. You will save lots of time while generating comparable returns.

The below shows a simple exercise I performed just to get my point across. I compared the top 10 dividend growers of Canadian public companies' total returns with some vanguard ETFs. The dividend growers are not too bad but not great for all the efforts you put in.

Name	Yrs of dividend increase	Returns		
		YTD	3-year	5-year
Canadian Utilities	46	-13%	1%	2%
Fortis	44	-5%	11%	10%
Canadian Western Bank	26	8%	20%	6%
Atco	24	-13%	4%	0%
Thomson Reuters	24	10%	8%	14%
Empire Company	23	3%	-4%	-1%
Imperial Oil	23	1%	-2%	-1%
Metro	23	2%	7%	14%
Canadian National Railway	22	11%	19%	19%
Enbridge	22	-5%	-1%	5%
	Dividend growers (Avg)	0%	6%	7%
	VTI (US)	2%	13%	9%
	VCE (Canada)	2%	9%	8%

That's it from me. Keep learning, watch your eggs, get rid of any weeds, find an investing style that fits you, save, invest and then rinse and repeat until you reach your goals. I will end this post with my one of favorite quotes. Forgot who said this but can't agree enough with what he/she said:

I love temporary problems because they typically provide the greatest buying opportunities. Half-seriously, I think that one of the best investment strategies could be to seek out great companies and then wish real hard that something bad happens to them – something temporarily bad, of course. When problems raise their head, Wall Street can be depended on to put a company on skewers and hold it over the fire, regardless of whether the problem is temporary or permanent.

10 Pieces of Advice to Save a lot of Time and a lot of Money When You Begin

By: Don't Fuck with Donville Blog

The hardest thing for new investors is to know where to invest. What's a good company? What's a good CEO? Both are very important, but, for beginners, they're both hard to evaluate. We can't know these things instinctually. That's why most people follow the first person they can: A journalist on TV, on a website, on the radio, a workmate or a neighbour. And there's no warranty of quality.

Your duty as an individual investor is to seek autonomy as soon as possible. I know it sucks, because we like to make as little effort as possible to get what we want. It's going to take years, but my advice is to read about the stock market like you would read about another topic of interest: rock and roll, movies, hockey, football, etc. You won't be good if you're not passionate about it. Nobody gets good at anything if they're not passionate about it.

If you don't get the autonomy I'm talking about, you'll be manipulated in a way or another. You'll read people trying to pump their penny stocks, which can be done easily if a moderate audience swallows everything they say. Or you'll buy the big names that analysts, sponsored by big companies, will try to sell you. These big names may not be bad picks, but they may not be great picks either.

You won't get that autonomy easily, so, if you find some people that look honest, stick with them for a while. There's not that many of these people in the investment world.

To help you a little, I have "5 never-invest rules" and "5

essentials to invest rules".

Let's begin with the "5 never-invest rules":

1. Never invest money in a stock where there's a lot of controversy;
2. Never invest money in a penny stock;
3. Never invest money in an industry which is declining;
4. Never invest money in natural resources;
5. Never invest money in a company that carries too much debt (e.g., 50% of their market cap or more)

And here's my "5 essentials to invest rules":

1. Search for stocks with a beta lower than 1 (lower than the market) (precision: many people seem to think that this metric is useless but I believe in it);
2. An historical return on equity (ROE) over than 15, and, ideally, higher than 20;
3. A forward PE between 15 and 25 (of course, if you pay 25 times next year's earnings, the growth has to be exceptional and the historical PE of the stock must have always been high);
4. Annual EPS growth of at least 10% over the last 5 years;
5. A high predictability of earnings.

If you apply the "5 never invest rules" and the "5 essentials to invest rules", I think that your chances of picking a great selection of stocks are high. I can't imagine someone going bankrupt while applying these 10 rules to a 15-20 stocks portfolio.

Rags to Riches (XPEL)
By: Max

In February 2013, XPEL caught my attention as it started to move up ever so slightly. On February 28, 2013, I bought 73,000 shares at $0.31. Why; several reasons:

1. Stock trending higher
2. Very clean company, no options or warrants and large insider position; roughly 30% +
3. Valuation was key; $0.31 x 25 million shares = $7,000,000 market cap
4. Superior software for the cutting of patterns

I rode the wave up and bought and sold till it peaked and turned down. I sold 150,000 shares in total till I was down to 48,000 shares at the end of Dec, 2017. Through 5 years of exceptional revenue growth, the growth didn't fall to the bottom line and the company was very tight lipped about anything they were doing.

The 3M lawsuit created another opportunity as investors threw in the towel and feared the company would even going out of business. In my search for alternative growth opportunities it brought me to people like Robin Speziale, Small Cap Discoveries, etc. When I compared many companies to XPEL, I found XPEL to be cheap on a revenue to market cap basis compared to 98% of all the other companies I came across.

Post settlement with 3M, I repurchased around 75,000 shares between $1.50 and $2.45. averaging around $2.00. I reinvested around $200,000 Canadian dollars because it was cheap. I did not know if XPEL could execute the business plan but my downside was covered in my opinion. By the way, XPEL did show up on Joel Greenblatt's screening as a value buy.

I am long 90% of my position still in XPEL. It has become a 7 figure valuation for me in Canadian dollars. All of the stock is in my RRSP and TFSA. So I'm not paying the taxman yet.

The lessons learned and employed were the following:

1. Valuation is key. Don't put yourself in a position to lose money, although frivolous lawsuits can be a hindrance. Understanding risk is key. Lessons taught by many. Howard Marks resonated with me on that particular point.

2. To make outsized profits, concentrated positions are necessary. Munger and Druckenmiller are examples.

3. Understand the company inside out. This I got lucky with as I was involved from the inception but I kept my eye on the ball the whole time.

4. Liquidate a position on the way down. This allowed me to sell 75% of the position before reloading. This is a Livermore rule. You never know where a top is but you can see it turn.

Always look at the alternatives to your position. When I sold on the way down, I took a very large position in Blackbird Energy at $.15 with warrants. I accumulated as the stock ran to $.70 and they did a financing at $.55 for $85 million. When I purchased Blackbird Energy, all they had was a land position. My purchase was predicated on risk. Land was worth the market cap of the company, in a hot area and with nobody paying attention. No revenue at all but lots of potential. Long and short of it is that with leverage from warrants I sold most of my stock at $.50 plus warrants at $.30 plus on a $.15 unit. I also bought stock and warrants on the way up. It was a tenbagger while I was waiting to reenter XPEL.

I don't ever believe I can do that again but it has been life changing for me. Part of it is being in the right place at the right time. So luck plays a part in it no doubt.

My Investment Checklist
By: Christopher Gimmer,
Co-founder of Snappa and Stockfox

Although I studied finance and accounting in university, I ended up stumbling my way into entrepreneurship. Nowadays, I spend the majority of my day working on my own business as opposed to analyzing the businesses of others. However, I feel like this has become an advantage, not a weakness.

As the great Warren Buffett once said:

"I am a better investor because I am a businessman, and I am a better businessman because I am an investor."

When I'm thinking about investing in a company, I put my business owner cap on before I ever look at a single financial statement. While many analysts focus heavily on numbers and ratios, I save most of the financial analysis for the end of my due diligence.

Here is the very first question that I'm trying to answer:

"Is this a good business?"

If it's a crappy business then I don't care if it's 'undervalued'. If stocks are 'undervalued', that means I need to determine what the fair value is, wait until the market catches up, then sell at the right time. While some people may be successful at this, I think it's becoming increasingly more difficult. After all, cheap stocks can get cheaper.

Instead, I'd rather invest in great businesses and hold them over long periods of time. As a retail investor, I believe that time is one of the biggest advantages that we have. Unlike institutional investing, we don't need to worry about performance over quarters, we only need to worry about performance over years and decades. This means that if we invest in truly great businesses, the stock should perform well given a long enough time horizon. I think that the market generally under-appreciates growth over the long term. Hence why great growth stocks are always considered 'overvalued'.

Since I'm exposed to a lot of products and services both as a business owner and as a consumer, most of my investments are in companies whose products & services I use, or have a deep understanding of. This makes it much easier to monitor my investments over time.

Evaluating the Strength of a Business

Although there isn't a definitive checklist that will tell you whether or not something is a great business, there are certainly indicators we can look for. Here are some of my favourite things to look for when evaluating businesses:

Does the company have pricing power?

Without a doubt, pricing power is one of the best attributes a business can have. All things being equal, higher prices lead to higher margins, higher profits, and the ability to re-invest more money back into the business.

One of my favourite companies with clear pricing power is Lululemon. At my gym, I typically see well over 50% of the women working out in Lululemon clothes despite the fact that it costs $98+ for a single pair of leggings.

Some of the greatest investments in recent memory like Amazon, Netflix and Apple have all displayed exceptional pricing power. No one bats an eye when the cost of

Amazon Prime or Netflix goes up, nor do people seem hesitant to drop over $1,000 on a new iPhone.

Does the company have sustainable competitive advantages?

Some people refer to this as a "moat." Essentially, I'm looking for characteristics of the business that will help fend off competition for years to come. Most people will bucket these into the following areas:

- Cost advantages
- Network effects
- High switching costs
- Intangible assets (Brand, patents, etc…)

Moats have been written about to death so I won't spend too much time on it here. I simply want to point out that a strong business should have at least 1 identifiable competitive advantage. Evidently, the more the better.

Is the business model built on repeat purchases?

As a SaaS founder myself, I know just how much easier it is to run a business when you're not starting from zero every month. This is why I love business models with recurring revenue and repeat purchases.

For non-SaaS businesses, I look for products that are 'sticky'. The more ingrained that product or service is into the daily lives of the customer, the better.

Is there opportunity for revenue expansion?

This is one of my favourite things to look for when I'm evaluating businesses, especially software companies. If the company generates more revenue from existing customers over time, I get really excited. This is why I love companies like Square who share in the upside of their customer base.

With SaaS companies in particular, I pay close attention to net dollar retention rates. A net dollar retention rate over 100% means the company is generating more revenue over time from their existing customer base, even when churn is factored in. The higher the lifetime value of the customer, the better.

Does the business have optionality?

I love investing in businesses that are able to continuously release new products and expand into other markets. For me, the more optionality the better.

Going back to Square, they started out as a simple hardware solution that let small merchants easily accept payments. Later, they added a variety of merchant solutions like Square Capital and Payroll. Most recently, they launched the Square Cash app which lets people send and receive payments and even buy Bitcoin. Square has now created a whole ecosystem around payments & services and will continue to have optionality going forward.

Additional questions

Beyond the major factors above, here are some additional questions I like to ask when evaluating the strength of the business:

- Does the company pass the 'snap' test (i.e., if the company disappeared tomorrow, would anybody care?)
- Does the company have a well-respected brand?
- Does the company have first mover advantage? (This doesn't always guarantee success)

- Is the company's customer base diversified?

Market Opportunity

Since I typically hold stocks over long periods of time, I only want to invest in companies that have a sizeable market opportunity ahead of them. That's not to say that everything I invest in needs to be growing at ridiculous pace, but I'm generally not interested in holding stocks with limited to no growth opportunities.

Although there are research reports and industry analyses that try to quantify the size of a market, I try not to get too bogged down in precise numbers. Rather, I focus on the big picture. It doesn't take huge in-depth analysis to realize that:

- We are moving to a cashless society
- Households are getting rid of cable TV
- eSports is booming
- AI is getting smarter
- Cars are becoming autonomous

When I spot a trend, I try to figure out which companies will benefit the most and invest accordingly.

Culture & Management

Once I identify a great business with a sizeable market opportunity, I then shift my focus towards culture and the management team.

Since company culture and visionary leadership doesn't show up on the financial statements of a company, this is another area where I think retail investors have an edge.

Admittedly, this is more of an art than science but here are some things that I look for...

Is the founder part of the management team or board of directors?

If a company founder has stayed on as CEO well after IPO, you can be reasonably assured that their heart is in it for the right reasons. I want to invest in leaders that care more about the mission of the company than their annual compensation.

Do employees like working there?

When the employees of a business are excited to show up to work regardless of compensation, that's when magic starts to happen. These employees will work a lot harder and smarter than unfulfilled employees.

To get a sense of employee happiness, I love to read employee reviews on Glassdoor.com. Although there's no doubt some fake reviews, I find the site gives a pretty good proxy about the employee sentiment of a company. If you know anyone that works at the company, ask them directly. After talking with many employees of Shopify and visiting their headquarters, it's quite clear that employees love working there!

Does the founder still hold a large stake in the company?

If the founder still holds on to a lot of stock, they clearly believe in the long term success of the business. Founders will no doubt sell off stock as time goes on but huge changes in ownership could (but not always) be a red flag.

Does the company have a broader purpose?

This one is a bit difficult to evaluate since even the worst companies will have some sort of generic mission statement that they pretend to believe in. However, you can usually decipher the fakers from the "truthers".

Most companies were started because the founders were passionate about solving a problem, not because they wanted to make a lot of money. I look for companies whose founders and employees are passionate about the company's mission and want to do right by their stakeholders.

Financials

Finally, we come to financials. At this point, I'm looking for the financial statements to back up my qualitative analysis above. If it is a great business, the numbers should reflect that.

Here are some things I look for when analyzing a company's financial statements:

Are sales growing?

When it comes to the best performing stocks, they typically have awesome rates of sales growth. All things being equal, the higher the growth the better.

Are margins expanding?

Here I'm looking for stable, and ideally expanding long-term margins. For companies that are not yet profitable, their operating expenses as a percentage of revenue should continue to decrease as the company scales, indicating a clear path to profitability.

Are they generating cash flow?

Cash is king. I want to invest in companies that generate a lot of it.

Do they have a strong balance sheet?

Here I'm looking for companies with lots of cash and little to no debt. I want to be assured that in tough times, the company won't evaporate. This is especially crucial for small cap stocks that are not yet profitable. For companies that do have debt, I want to ensure their debt levels are serviceable.

Some other things I look at:

- Does the business have a high ROE?
- Are they investing adequately in R&D?
- Are shares outstanding holding steady?

There's a million things one can look for when analyzing financial statements and entire books have been written about it. In a nutshell, I'm verifying that the company is growing sales, expanding margins, generating cash, and has a strong balance sheet.

Summary

Putting it all together, I want to invest in a great business, in a growing market, with a strong culture and sound financials.

When I find these types of investments, I hold them over long periods of time and let the returns continue to compound for years or decades.

Interview with Philippe Bergeron-Bélanger – Micro Cap Investor

By: Philippe Bergeron-Bélanger,
Co-founder of ESPACE MicroCaps and
Consultant for Rivemont MicroCap Fund

What's your background?

I'm 31, live in Montreal and have been a full time investor since August 2014. Currently, I'm a Consultant for the Rivemont MicroCap Fund. I have a background in finance and accounting. Out of University, I started to work at Travelers Canada as an underwriter. In 2013, one of my colleague there introduced me to microcaps and told me about two companies that were growing over 50% per year and trading at 10 times earnings. I decided to buy positions and they both went up multiple times in the following year.

Needless to say, I was hooked. In August 2014, I decided to quit my job to become a full-time microcap investor and never looked back.

As the last few years went by, Mathieu and I got well-known in the microcap space thanks to the quality of our stock picks on the blog and the solid track-record we achieved. Many of our friends and family members started to ask us to manage their money, which was very exciting.

The problem was that we didn't have a portfolio management license and it is something mandatory to manage other people's money in Canada. In 2018, we decided to join an asset management firm called Rivemont as consultants to launch the Rivemont MicroCap Fund. The firm is very innovative and seeks to offer many non-traditional investment products, which is something we fit into and want to develop further. The MicroCap Fund is now running since January and we provide the portfolio manager with all of our fundamental research and best investment ideas. We are also heavily invested in the Fund alongside the other investors.

Tell me about your investing style and influences:

Interestingly, I made some money playing poker while I was in University. The biggest takeaway from this experience was the importance of having sound decision-making processes and the discipline to stick to them. It helped me to detach myself emotionally from money, and start thinking in terms of risks, rewards and expected returns. As an investor, the goal should be to maximize the potential return per unit of risk. Some prefer to minimize the downside first (think "margin of safety") and then find the best investment opportunities for that level of risk.

Others prefer to focus on the highest potential return only. I would say I am a proponent of the former more than the latter.

What's your overall strategy in the micro-cap space?

I always ran a concentrated portfolio of Canadian microcaps and that is still what I recommend to the Rivemont MicroCap Fund. My goal is to find undervalued and undiscovered equities that have the potential to at least double in a 2 to 3 years' timeframe. In a nutshell, I look for mispriced growth stocks because I can make money in two ways: 1) Growing revenues and EPS and 2) Expansion of the valuation multiple.

Describe your stock selection process.

I look for growth businesses that present as much of the following attributes as possible (or have the potential to show them in a relatively short timeframe):

- Strong revenue growth (typically 25%+ year over year)
- High gross margins (typically 50% or more) and/or high asset turnover
- Operating leverage (expanding GM% and EBITDA%)
- Cash flow positive from operations
- Positive working capital and minimal debt
- Clean share structure with low dilution risk from options and warrants
- High insider ownership (ideally a founder-operated business)
- Low institutional ownership
- No analyst coverage
- Low customer concentration risk
- Some sort of niche competitive advantages and/or intellectual property

I don't tend to put a lot of weight on past performance as most microcaps are too early stage or have struggled for many years before showing glimpses of hope. If they were solid businesses, they wouldn't be microcaps after all. In other words, I can get comfortable with only a few quarters of sound financial performance as long as I pay a reasonable-to-cheap price given the growth potential of the company. I generally avoid natural resources, biotech, pot and finance companies because they don't meet enough of my investment criteria.

Tell me about your risk management tactics.

The best risk-mitigating activity is to do a lot more research than anyone else. You want to get an informational edge on other investors before you invest and after. Before initiating a position, I almost always speak with the management team and try to gather as much information as possible to make better decisions. If you know what you own better than most other investors, you should understand where the risks might come from and react appropriately (and quickly) when things go south. The bottom line is that you need to follow your positions closely.

What are your annual returns?

My TFSA is a good indicator of my past performance. I've been investing for 5 years now and my capital has grown more than 10 times the maximum contribution room.

Do you have some advice and outlook for DIY investors?

1. Companies that are dominating a niche tend to do better than those chasing large opportunities. They run a profitable business in their niche and can reinvest profits to expand their total addressable market.

2. Turn off the noise, stop listening to mainstream media and focus on finding companies that should do well in any macro environment. Remember that the price you pay is your margin of safety.

3. Don't use leverage. If it's not good for the companies you invest in, it shouldn't be good for you either.

What's a great investing book you've read that isn't mainstream?

Insider Buy Superstocks: The Super Laws of How I Turned $46K into $6.8 Million (14,972%) in 28 Months by Jesse Stine

How to Evaluate a Public Company in Thirty Minutes (Or Less)

By: Mathieu Martin,
Co-founder of ESPACE MicroCaps and
Consultant for Rivemont MicroCap Fund

What should you do when you discover a new company that you think might be interesting? Where should you start to determine whether this is a good opportunity or not?

Nowadays, it is relatively easy to be exposed to new investment ideas on a regular basis, whether it be on social media, message boards, email, YouTube, conferences or other networking events, etc. If you are like me and your watch list is already very large (maybe even too large), you need a process to quickly determine if a company deserves your attention or not. Over time, I developed a personal routine that allows me to get a good overview of a business in 30 minutes or less in order to see if it meets enough of my investment criteria. If that's the case, I'll add it to my watch list and spend more time on it later, otherwise I'll dismiss it immediately.

Is this technique perfect and does it prevent me from missing any good opportunities? Of course not. But since my time is limited and I will never get to know all North American microcap companies, I need to filter as efficiently as possible. Here's an overview of my process:

Step #1: Financial Statements

I like to start with financial statements because it's a quick way for me to filter out a number of companies that do not fit my criteria. You can find the financial statements (and all other official documents) of Canadian-listed companies on Sedar.com. Some of the things I typically look for:

- Does the company have revenue? Is it growing?
- Is the company profitable or about to reach profitability?
- Is the balance sheet healthy?
- How many shares are outstanding and what is the market cap?

Many times, my research ends at this stage, especially if the company has no revenue and/or burns through a lot of cash every quarter. If the balance sheet is in poor shape, for example showing a large working capital deficit or a considerable amount of debt, I may also not be very enthusiastic to keep searching.

Step #2: The Company's Website

After I see some potential, or at least didn't see anything that turned me off in the financial statements, I usually go to the company's website. My main objective is to find an investor presentation (PDF or PowerPoint document) in the investor section of the website. I would say I generally find such a document 50% to 75% of the time.

The investor presentation is typically a 20 to 30 page document that provides an overview of the business. This allows me to quickly understand what kind of products or services the company sells, what industry it's in, what are some of the highlights that make it a good investment opportunity (according to the management team), etc. After the quantitative analysis of step #1, I now focus on the qualitative aspect during step #2.

If I didn't manage to find an investor presentation, I will quickly browse the website to take a look at the products or services offered. I will also read the management team and board of directors bios to learn more about their experience.

Step #3: The Management Discussion & Analysis (MD&A)

The MD&A is a document that is systematically filed together with quarterly or annual financial statements, and it's also available on Sedar.com. The MD&A essentially is a detailed review of the financial statements with commentary from the management team. It includes a description of the company and, if applicable, its various subsidiaries, an overview of the industry, the company's growth strategy, an in-depth review of financial results as well as risk factors to consider before investing.

Several companies also include a section called "Outlook" and this is often the one that provides the best insights when it comes to filtering quickly. In this section, management shares details about the company's future prospects and main goals for the upcoming months or years. The language used in this section often reveals positive or negative clues that help me understand whether the business is experiencing positive momentum or is going through tough times.

Step #4: The Most Recent Press Releases

Again using Sedar.com, I take a look at the last 5 to 10 press releases to see what were the most important announcements in recent months. Also, if a material news item has been published recently, the company may not have had the time to include it in its investor presentation or in the MD&A. This step allows me to make sure I have a complete picture of what's been happening and where the company is now.

Bonus Steps

If I have time left or want to know a little more immediately, I like to take a look at the following:

Average daily trading volume on the stock: This allows me to get a feel for how much the company is known by other investors. The more volume, the more likely it's well-known. I prefer when a stock is illiquid (doesn't trade a lot), which means it's likely to be under the radar and unknown by other investors. If a company is unknown, my odds of finding an undervalued and potentially attractive investment opportunity are improved.

Insider ownership: I like when the management team and the board of directors own a significant stake in the company, which incentivizes them to act in the best interests of shareholders. The level of insider ownership can sometimes be found in the investor presentation. Otherwise, you'll have to go to SEDI.ca and manually calculate it. Warning: SEDI is not very user-friendly and the website seems like it hasn't been updated for decades!

Blog posts or analyst reports: If I can get my hands on detailed analyzes of the company published by bloggers or analysts, this can make my due diligence process much easier. On the other hand, the easier my job is, the easier it is for other investors as well. When I cannot find any article about the company and there is no analyst coverage, my odds of finding a bargain increase dramatically.

Now What?

As a result of this short process, I usually have a good idea if the company appears to have potential or not. For example, I might have been impressed by revenue growth (Step #1) or a product/service that looks very promising (Step #2). I could also just be interested based on traditional value investing metrics such as a low price/book ratio. Whatever the reason, I must feel curious to dig a little further. When a company has passed this first filter successfully, I will include it in my watch list and subscribe to Conference Call Transcripts updates to receive all the new Sedar documents that the company will publish in the future.

Subsequently, my due diligence process generally involves building a financial model and making revenue forecasts, doing a peer analysis as well as a thorough assessment of risks and potential catalysts. After a good in-depth research, I typically try to get in touch with management to ask some of the questions I didn't find answers to during my research. I may spend dozens of hours of research before being comfortable enough to make an investment.

That being said, the four-step process explained in this chapter allows me to filter most new businesses in about 30 minutes and to avoid spending dozens of hours researching opportunities that are not worth it. I encourage you to develop your own process by incorporating your criteria and identifying the essential ingredients you want to find in order to make an investment.

How to Conduct a CEO Interview
(Example – Good Natured Products)
By: Zachary Trease, Bizy Beaver

I first looked for the CEO's contact info but couldn't find it. So I emailed Investors Relations with 3 primary questions, bolding the most important parts so they could respond quickly. They hadn't responded after 2 weeks so I followed up and asked if I could have the CEO's direct email.

On that email, I cc'd paul@goodnatured.ca. I completely guessed his email address, but a day later he responded answering all my questions (I had guessed right!). He was so excited to hear from an investor and asked me to spread the word, even offering to talk over the phone for further questions and asked to add me to his investor list.

I got all my questions answered and now am a well-informed owner of the company.

This is another Canadian micro-cap that I allocated a SMALL position to. They've got motivated leadership with a great brand and business model while riding not only the very hot packaging industry, but more specifically, the plant-based packaging industry. In today's environmentally-focused culture, this is at the forefront of many people's minds. I managed to contact GDNP's CEO with some questions, with his answers in bold as follows:

Aside from being environmentally conscious, are there other motivating factors for your customers to use good natured packaging (especially since I assume there is some cost premium to traditional plastics)?

Our packaging designs play a big role as we do have

some proprietary packaging designs. I also want to note that our packaging is NOT priced at a premium to petroleum packaging. A matter of fact many times we are priced the same and or better then petroleum. I attached our herb packaging collateral as an example [see attached]. We send this out to herb growers to let them know the switching is very easy and no additional cost to them, ie same price for our package as their current Petroleum package.

I know it's something more and more consumers care about, but my concern is that it's not obvious that a certain product is made from plant-based plastic. Do your customers advertise the plant-based aspect? Is there some sort of universally-recognized label?

Our packaging is branded 99% plant base - good natured on the bottom. Our customers do communicate through social media, press releases, and in store. In some cases they put it on the label. No universal code exists for plant base packaging but the recycling symbol used today for plant base packaging is 7. Canada and the USA are considering creating a separate symbol for plant base packaging material)

What division of good natured does the executive team perceive to have the most potential? In other words, what is the company's primary focus? I could not find a revenue breakdown by division.

Our focus is to detoxify the kitchen, so any packaging and or product that is used or finds its way into the kitchen is our target. Our Packaging business group is the most important)

How competitive is this space? Two companies I came across were Vegware and NatureWorks, but I'm sure there are others. How will customers differentiate between you and your competitors?

99.5% of the time we compete against petroleum packaging, the other .5% is fiber board. Natureworks is one of many plant base material ingredient companies. They are not a direct competitor. A matter of fact we have a very strong relationship with them as they are one of our ingredient suppliers. I know Vegwar well. They compete in the food service segment, which we current do no business in. Yet :-) They would be considered a competitor to watch for us)

Does good natured have an advantage in Canada over these (and other) companies?

Good natured has created a very large competitive advantage against future plant base companies and petroleum packaging companies. Our competitive advantages include, (1) having over 130 different products provides us price and authority advantage. If you want to start a company to compete against our 130 products it would require over $10 million USD just to make the molds, (2) patented material composite IP, (3) patented packaging designs, exclusive supplier agreements, diverse customer mix, and manufacturing scalability).

Also, do note that there are some downsides to plant-based packaging, and they certainly aren't the perfect replacement to regular plastic as summarized here. But they are a step forward in the right direction and industry giants such as Hasbro recognize this.

Some other points from this presentation:

- Insiders and management own 45%
- Bioplastics industry is estimated to grow up to 30% CAGR (heavy industry tailwinds)
- Paul (CEO) is the former CEO of Best Buy's European operations
- Paul expects GDNP to continue growing revenue at least 50% per year

Paul says they can grow into a $100M revenue company without any further capital expenditures because their supply chain (manufacturing, engineering, logistics etc.) is outsourced, and further they are also investors in GDNP (own 13%). This also allows them to create highly customizable solutions.

100+ DIY INVESTOR RESOURCES

These are some of my favourite resources that can help you on your DIY Investing journey – analysis, news, and more

Stock Analysis (Data, Screens and Charts):

- Yahoo Finance
- Morningstar
- Finviz
- TMX Money
- TradingView
- CapitalCube
- StockWatch
- StockCharts
- BigCharts
- YCharts

Research:

- SeekingAlpha
- WhaleWisdom
- Investopedia
- Dataroma
- Investcom Market Insights
- GuruFocus
- Valueline Investment Survey
- Validea

- Baystreet.ca (New Listings)

Forums:

- StockChase
- StockHouse
- StockFox
- Corner of Berkshire and Fairfax
- Motley Fool
- Reddit

Tracking / Watchlist:

- StockMarket App
- Yahoo Finance
- Investing.com

Financial News:

- BNN
- Bloomberg
- Reuters
- MarketWatch
- Financial Times
- Financial Post
- Report on Business
- Twitter
- Wall Street Journal
- SmallCapPower
- Reuters
- Zack's Investment Research
- ZeroHedge

- Kiplinger

Financial Statements:

- SEDAR
- EDGAR
- Companies' websites
- BamSEC
- QuantumOnline
- Canadian Investor
- Canadian Insider
- Conference Call Transcripts

Investment Blogs:

- Be Smart Rich
- Don't Fuck with Donville
- The Stock Market Speculator
- Base Hit Investing
- Investorfile
- Thelongtrend.com
- InvestorsFriend.com/zachs-research
- QualitySmallCaps.com
- The GARP Investor
- The Greater Fool
- The Sassy Investor
- Espace MicroCaps
- RAE-Plutus-Normative
- #investing
- 25iq

- A Wealth of Common Sense
- Value Walk
- Small Cap Discoveries
- Abnormal Returns
- Investment Talk (SPBrunner)
- Aswath Damodaran
- Canadian Value Stocks

Stock Market Movies:

- Wall Street
- The Wolf of Wall Street
- Inside Job
- The Big Short
- Margin Call
- Boiler Room

Financial Podcasts:

- Invest Like the Best
- The Meb Faber Show
- Focus Compounding
- Planet Money
- How I Built This
- $100 MBA Show
- The Wise Investor Show
- The Investors Podcast
- Rule Breaker Investing
- Tropical MBA
- Y Combinator

- Startups for the Rest of Us
- Mixergy
- Indie Hackers
- Success! How I Did It
- Planet MicroCap

Investment Funds & Companies (study their holdings)

- Berkshire Hathaway
- 3G Capital
- Sequoia Fund
- SQ Advisors
- Third Point
- Markel Corp
- Brave Warrior Advisors LLC
- Gotham Funds
- Akre Capital Management
- Hillside Wealth Management
- Donville Kent Asset Management
- Giverny Capital
- Fundsmith
- Light Street Capital Management
- Turtle Creek Asset management
- Mawer New Canada Fund
- PenderFund Capital Management
- Pershing Square
- Cascade Investment
- Oakmark Fund

- Icahn Enterprises
- Oaktree Capital
- Kynikos Associates
- Fidelity (Canadian Growth Fund)
- Himalaya Capital
- Elliott Management
- Arlington Value

More Books on Growth Investing

- How to Make Money in Stocks, William O'Neil
- The Little Book That Beats the Market, Joel Greenblatt
- How I Made $2,000,000 in the Stock Market, Nicolas Darvas
- How to Make Money in Stocks: Getting Started, Matthew Galgani
- Reminiscences of a Stock Operator, Edwin Lefevre
- Insider Buy Superstocks, Jesse C. Stine
- Martin Zweig's Winning on Wall Street, Martin Zweig
- You Can Be a Stock Market Genius, Joel Greenblatt
- 100 Baggers, Christopher Mayer
- 100 to 1 in the Stock Market, Thomas William Phelps
- The Outsiders: Eight Unconventional CEOs and Their Radically Rational Blueprint for Success, William N. Thorndike
- Zero to One: Notes on Startups, or How to Build the Future, Peter Thiel

ABOUT THE AUTHOR

Robin R. Speziale
r.speziale@gmail.com | RobinRSpeziale.com

Robin R. Speziale (born August 6, 1987) is a DIY Investor and Globe and Mail National Bestselling Author; *Market Masters* (2016). He won the Independent Publisher Book Award for Finance/Investment/Economics. Robin has been investing in the stock market since 2005, and built a $300,000+ portfolio before 30. Mr. Speziale lives in Toronto, Ontario. Visit RobinRSpeziale.com and email Robin – r.speziale@gmail.com. If you live in and around Toronto, grab a coffee with Robin.

ACKNOWLEDGEMENTS

To –

Family: Mom, Dad, and Sister.

Grandparents: rest in peace.

All of my relatives: in Canada, Sweden, Italy, USA.

Friends. Teachers. Readers.

Thank you.

BUY MARKET MASTERS

Buy my National Bestselling Book, Market Masters:
Interview with Canada's Top Investors, on Amazon

There is nothing like *Market Masters* for the Canadian "Do it Yourself" (DIY) investor. Before I wrote the book, I would browse the Business / Investing bookshelves at my local Indigo, Chapters, and Coles book stores and only find investing books written by Americans for Americans. Sure, there are lots of Canadian books on personal finance, budgeting, saving, how to get started investing, mutual funds, etc. but those do not count. Especially any book that promises "sleep easy investing"… (*yawn*) or that teaches "investing for dummies". I'm talking about Canadian books on good old stock picking. There was nothing.

That's why I wrote *Market Masters*.

I wanted to create a go-to manual for Canadian DIY investors, featuring the top investors from across the country, their stock picking strategies, spanning different investing styles, and packing it all into 600 pages.

So, I started on the book-writing journey. I wrote the first draft of *Market Masters* in 2015, drawing material from my interviews with 28 top Canadian investors, and then shopping the manuscript around to ~50 publishers. They all rejected *Market Masters*. Most rejection emails were automated, but some were typed up by someone at the respective publishing house. For example, one editor flat out said, "Your book won't sell". Another explained that "People would rather read this type of content in magazines". It wasn't until I sent the manuscript to ECW Press that *Market Masters* found a home. The publisher's founder, Jack David, saw the potential in *Market Masters*. He believed in me, my book, and the value it would bring to DIY investors across the country. There truly wasn't anything like it. *Market Masters* released nationwide, in stores and online on February '16, and then two months later, became both a Globe and Mail and Toronto Star National Bestseller. It's been read by thousands of DIY investors across the country. And it's quickly becoming one of the most popular Canadian investing books of all time.

Here's what one reader said about *Market Masters*: "While America has a healthy supply of financial authors, Canada's under covered market is lucky to have someone like Robin Speziale. Just as Jack Schwager authored multiple editions in his Market Wizard series, so too should Robin with a Market Masters series". Another reader said: "This book is the best investment I ever made! I am on my second reading. Lots of great ideas concerning how to invest in the market. Diverse opinions and lots of examples. It was interesting to read how these Marketing Masters go about choosing the stocks they do."

I hope that you enjoy *Market Masters*. I think you'll gain an edge in the market after you read it if you haven't done so already. Pick up the book from Amazon.

THANKS FOR READING!

I WANT TO STAY CONNECTED WITH YOU, AND SEND YOU NEW CONTENT, FREEBIES, AND MY 15 BEST NEW STOCK IDEAS FOR THE NEW YEAR.

HOW TO STAY IN TOUCH:

SUBSCRIBE TO MY INVESTMENT NEWSLETTER (JOIN 3,500+ SUBSCRIBERS)

IT'S FREE!

GO TO:

ROBINSPEZIALE.COM/SUBSCRIBE

OR

EMAIL ME: R.SPEZIALE@GMAIL.COM

CPSIA information can be obtained
at www.ICGtesting.com
Printed in the USA
LVHW090521081118
596414LV00002B/467/P